GLOBAL SOURCING

Lee Krotseng

PT Publications, Inc.
3109 45th Street, Suite 100
West Palm Beach, FL 33407-1915

Library of Congress Cataloging in Publication Data

Krotseng, Lee, 1942-
    Global sourcing / Lee Krotseng.
           p.   cm.
      Includes index.
      ISBN 0-945456-42-5 (pb)
      1. Industrial procurement--Management.   I. Title
    HD39.5.K76   1997
    658.7'2--dc20   96-30413
                                                          CIP

Copyright © 1997 by PT Publications, Inc.

Printed in the United States of America

TABLE OF CONTENTS

To my wife, Marsha, whose encouragement, support and belief in me made this book possible. And to R & B who made sure I kept my sense of humor and my feet firmly planted in reality while I was writing this book.
LEE

PREFACE

At Pro-Tech, we have been educating and counseling all of our clients about the criticality of sourcing in an era when procurement of supplies has become increasingly important. Lee Krotseng has extended our range to include sourcing on an international scale. His book dovetails very well with a number of our other books on purchasing, particularly *Just-In-Time Purchasing: In Pursuit of Excellence* and *Supplier Certification II: A Handbook for Achieving Excellence Through Continuous Improvement*, both from PT Publications. Both of these books, as well as this one which you are about to read, place an emphasis on win/win relationships with suppliers.

Suppliers know their business. If you don't trust your suppliers, then why are you dealing with them? Given that they know what they are doing, it is reasonable to seek their advice and tap their expertise. From now on, when you sit down with suppliers and give them a list of your needs, seek out and listen to their feedback. Make them understand that a partnership is not only essential to the demands of frequent, small, defect-free deliveries in a JIT/TQC relationship, but will benefit them as much as it does you. In effect, you are telling your suppliers that you will commit your company to a long-term relationship, if they are willing to commit their companies to the practices and philosophies of JIT/TQC.

Separating the wheat from the chaff, the good supplier from the bad, has been, and will always remain, an important duty of purchasing. Indeed, supplier selection may even gain in importance, since single and sole suppliers are not unheard of and are even desirable.

The aim is not to favor one sourcing philosophy over another, but to be flexible in selecting sources. We have found that most companies need to reduce dramatically the number of suppliers they use. Single-sourcing through Supplier Certification is the most desirable way to achieve this reduction. Subsequently, it is no longer our role simply to get the best price and handle all the clerical work associated with buying. As part of a company-wide team, especially linked with planning, Purchasing must find suppliers willing and capable of meeting the demands of Total Quality Control and of putting in place and maintaining strict manufacturing process controls. If the world was a neat and tidy place, you would only need to go out shopping at various factories where you could inspect their "labels" and see who has what you want. But, sourcing requires looking beyond labels.

There are three areas of information to study when selecting suppliers. They are:

1. **Objective performance data.**
2. **Long-term vitality and financial responsibility.**
3. **Technical leadership and know-how.**

The Buyer/Planners then look at the supplier base and with these areas in mind ask the following questions about each supplier:

1. **Where are the suppliers located?**
2. **How many items does each supply?**
3. **What is their quality capability?**
4. **What is the supplier's delivery performance?**
5. **What are their min./max. capacity limits?**
6. **How responsive is the supplier to change?**

With the information contained in this book, you will be able to answer these questions. Lee Krotseng has written a guide which will help you understand the complex activities of sourcing in today's global marketplace.

Peter L. Grieco, Jr.
West Palm Beach, FL

ABOUT THE AUTHOR

Lee Krotseng, C.P.M. is Manager of Seminars and training for International Purchasing Service, a supplier of temporary purchasing/materials professionals and purchasing /materials consulting and training services based in Detroit Michigan. He has over sixteen years of purchasing and materials management experience from small startups to divisions of Fortune 500 companies. He has a Master's Degree in Industrial Management. He is the author of several articles on purchasing and Materials management. Lee has also taught college-level courses in purchasing and computer applications for business. He has presented seminars and is a frequent speaker on purchasing and materials management topics to N.A.P.M. affiliates nationwide. Lee is currently the Professional Development Chairperson and C.P.M. Study Review instructor for N.A.P.M. Tri-State. He can be reached by email at:
internet:76353.2035@compuserve.com.

ACKNOWLEDGMENTS

Many people (bosses, peers, and customers) have helped me develop and use the ideas contained in this book. While the list is too long to note everyone, several deserve special mention. Dale Reynolds, a true purchasing professional, acted as my sounding board and helped me clarify the book's framework, as well as provided valuable international experience and insight. Ron Gillian, another purchasing professional (whom I met in cyberspace and later in person), helped with the electronic commerce and Internet topics.

My thanks and appreciation to a former boss, Vince Ciarpella, who taught a new purchasing manager several lasting lessons about what top management wanted and needed from the purchasing function. I'd also like to thank my current boss, Tom Kaucic, for his support during the writing of this book. Thanks also to my editor, Steven Marks, for his creative editorial assistance.

EARLY INVOLVEMENT

CHAPTER ONE

Before a purchasing agent identifies possible sources of supply, he or she must first define the need. Purchase Requisitions, MRP Shortage Reports, Capital Asset Requisitions, Traveling Requisitions and Bar Code Requisitions, backed up by signature authorization procedures, are typically used to authorize the buyer to purchase a service or commodity. At a minimum, the requisition should answer these questions:

1) **What is needed?**
2) **When is it needed?**
3) **Who needs it?**

If available, additional information such as approved or preferred suppliers and target pricing can also be helpful.

What Is Needed?

Existing Goods and Services

Standard "off-the-shelf" goods for existing products and services are usually available from several suppliers and normally do not require much time to source. On the other hand, "one-of-a-kind" products or services may require a great deal of time to source. It is easy to find suppliers who can supply a standard magic marker. It may not be as easy to find a marker that can write 200 feet underwater. Generally speaking, the more complex the part, the greater the effort needed to find good sources of supply. The obvious exception to this rule may be the sole source product. (Note: A good buyer will always be looking for alternative suppliers — whether sole source or otherwise.)

New Products

Purchasing for new products usually requires significantly more purchasing time to identify sources of supply than do existing products. Unless an Early Supplier Involvement (ESI) program has been used which gets suppliers involved at the design phase, all new parts will require sourcing. In some cases, this may simply mean obtaining bids from existing suppliers. In other cases, a full-blown sourcing exercise, including identifying new sources of supply, supplier visits, bidding and supplier evaluation, may be necessary.

When Is It Needed?

A well-run purchasing operation will have procedures in place to handle standard sourcing and emergency sourcing. If the goods or services requested are within "normal lead-times" (ex: MRP production requirements), then sourcing decisions can be handled following standard sourcing procedures of selecting sources (usually sources already existing), obtaining bids, evaluating the bids, etc.

Short lead-time or "emergency" purchases of goods and services can force the buyer to depart from standard sourcing. If a production line is down due to a broken bearing, taking the time to get three bids before placing an order could get a buyer fired. Even Federal, State and Local governments in "state-of-emergency" situations waive the three bid rule. (During the rioting at the Democratic convention in Chicago, police required more handcuffs than were available. A local telephone employee gave the police some large plastic tie bands to use as a substitute. The next day a buyer for the telephone company received a requisition from the local government for large tie bands — due IMMEDIATELY!)

Who Needs It?

It is obvious that the "What" and "When needed" will impact a buyer's sourcing decision. It may not be as obvious that the type of organization and the "Who needs it?" questions will also significantly affect the buyer's options. Who Purchasing's customer is for a given requisition or requirement is not just a TQM exercise or an idle question. Each customer's needs are different and may vary from requisition to requisition, therefore each customer may need different emphasis. Sometimes the need may be tactical — for example, a bearing for a production machine. Other times the need may be for strategic sourcing of materials — coal for a power plant is a good example.

The following illustrations are three graphics of internal customers for a manufacturing organization, a retail/warehouse organization, and a public or governmental organization. Figure 1-1 shows a typical manufacturing organization chart. The reader's organization may have different reporting lines of authority, but all manufacturing organizations have the basic functions of Production, Accounting, Sales, Engineering, and Quality. Figures 1-2 and 1-3 do not have the production function, but are very similar to Figure 1-1. For example, all three must purchase office supplies. Each function will have different missions and emphases (some which may clash). Let's examine the sourcing needs for each function.

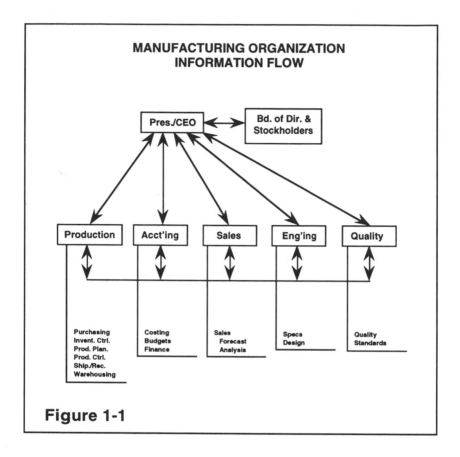

Figure 1-1

Sourcing Needs for Production

The production function needs dependable sources of supply to provide an uninterrupted flow of materials to the production process. This is true for Maintenance, Repair and Operating items, as well as component and piece parts. Quality is also important to keep rework and line down problems to a minimum. Cost is of lesser importance to many production functions.

Dependability is usually defined as on-time delivery — that is, the supplier delivers good product on the agreed upon dates. A source can also be considered dependable if it is willing to be flexible and to change scheduling to meet the ebb and flow of the

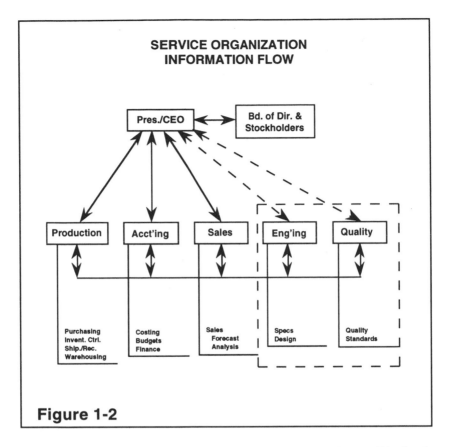

SERVICE ORGANIZATION INFORMATION FLOW

Figure 1-2

production process. In the best of all worlds, a supplier will be both flexible and meet its delivery dates. This is the concept behind approved supplier programs. Sometimes two or more suppliers are necessary to assure an uninterrupted supply to the production line, particularly if the production process is dynamic and subject to changes in a short period of time. A dependable source would also help Production to maximize each direct labor dollar by avoiding stockout situations due to late delivery or poor quality.

Sourcing Decisions for Engineering

Engineering and Research & Development functions are usu-

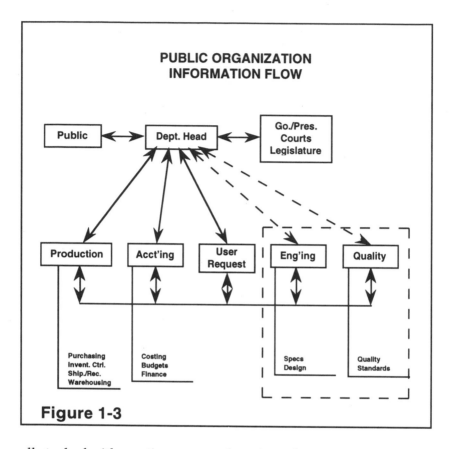

Figure 1-3

ally tasked with creating new products in as short a time as possible, utilizing the latest technology. This is true for a range of products from high-tech electronics to hand tools. Many times, the cost of an item is not as important to engineering as its availability and how fast it can be delivered for prototyping, evaluation and testing. Sources that can deliver immediately may not be the preferred sources to handle future production requirements. Engineering has a reputation for over-designing products. This can increase costs at the production end which will then clash with Purchasing's task to minimize total cost.

Ideally, Purchasing and Engineering should work together as part of a cross-functional team. This team would design a product that is value-engineered with supplier involvement on the front end (Early Supplier Involvement programs, etc.). This process helps create a smooth transition from prototype to full production. In some of the more well-run companies, this is exactly what happens and sourcing selections are made during the design phase by the team.

Sourcing Decisions for Quality

The Quality function is interested in obtaining goods or services that can be purchased at the lowest cost to meet the need or satisfy the function specified. Much of the time, documentation certifying compliance to process or drawing specifications is necessary to help assure proper quality. Quality requirements for goods and services must be designed in before identifying sources of supply. For example, if a machine part requires tolerances of .0001, then considering suppliers who consistently do work at tolerances of .001 is a waste of time.

Sourcing Decisions for Accounting and Other Support Services

The needs of Accounting and other support services for goods and services are usually not as immediate as Production or Engineering. However, sourcing decisions can be as critical to the smooth operation of the support services as decisions made for Production. For example, suppliers of accounting software must be able to meet specifications and requirements for reliability. Let's face it, no one wants a paycheck generated that doesn't calculate pay consistently and correctly due to "computer software" errors. Accounting usually wants whatever is purchased to be the lowest cost available to do the job. The same is true for most other departments or functions.

Sourcing for Sales

Sales or Marketing expects Purchasing to buy materials and services at the lowest total cost so that the organization can be competitive with other firms. Sales isn't as concerned as the Production function with day-to-day tactical buying. Its needs are more strategic. For example, Sales does want to know what the cost and delivery trends are for major material cost items so it can make pricing and delivery date adjustments. This is obvious. What is not as obvious, but is increasingly important for firms doing business in the worldwide marketplace is countertrade. According to a 1993 Center for Advanced Purchasing Study ("CEOs'/Presidents' Perceptions and Expectations of the Purchasing Function"), 49% of presidents and CEOs expect Purchasing to have major participation or contribution to international sourcing. An additional 29% expect Purchasing to have some input. Only 22% expect Purchasing to have no input.[1]

Sourcing for Top Management

CEOs, presidents, governors and others in top management also expect their purchasing departments to locate and use the best cost sources of supply. According to the study cited above, the purchasing function is expected to have a major contribution or participation in material quality management, international sourcing, strategic development and long-term planning.[2] Note that these are all strategic functions. The book *Power Purchasing* (PT Publications) discusses these cutting-edge issues for the 21st century in great detail.

"Best Cost" is a concept that has been around for many years. For example, Emerson Electric was using the idea in the 1980s. In the 1990s, it was recognized that all costs (quality, inventory, unit, obsolescence, etc.) were not being considered. The concept of Total or Activity Based Costing (sometimes also called Lifetime or Lifecycle Costing) is being considered by many manufacturing organizations. A total Best Cost source or producer is one that produces a product that meets all the specifications at the lowest delivered cost over the product's life-span. Some life-spans are very short — in some cases less than one year (ex: personal computers) while others may last up to ten years (ex: automotive parts). These elements should be considered when making sourcing decisions for your organization.

CEOs expect Purchasing to be involved in long-term planning (supplier partnerships, long-term contracts, etc.) particularly for "strategic materials" where shortages or price fluctuations can create significant problems.

Conclusion

1) **What is needed?**
2) **When is it needed?**
3) **Who needs it?**

To start sourcing without answering these questions can cause the buyer to make unwise decisions that can cost his or her organization time or money. Once these questions are answered, the buyer can proceed with his or her sourcing exercise.

[1]   "CEOs'/President's Perceptions and Expectations of the Purchasing Function" by William A. Bales, C.P.M., and Harold E. Feron, Ph.D., C.P.M. 1993., National Association of Purchasing Management, Center for Advanced Purchasing Studies.

[2]   "CEOs'/President's Perceptions and Expectations of the Purchasing Function" by William A. Bales, C.P.M., and Harold E. Feron, Ph.D., C.P.M. 1993., National Association of Purchasing Management, Center for Advanced Purchasing Studies.

INTERNAL
CONSIDERATIONS
AFFECTING THE
SOURCING DECISION

CHAPTER TWO

Most organizations have internal considerations that will affect the sourcing decision. Internal polices, the number of suppliers, strategic sourcing alliances or agreements, Early Supplier Involvement programs, policies concerning new vs. current suppliers, and how centralized or decentralized the purchasing operation is structured can dramatically influence or constrain a buyer's sourcing decisions. For example, if the buyer's organization has a strategic agreement to purchase all crystal oscillators from one supplier, then all requirements for crystal oscillators will be placed with that supplier. Each of the above mentioned considerations should be considered before the buyer starts a sourcing exercise. Let's examine each consideration more closely.

Internal Policies

Many organizations have internal policies that will affect the sourcing decision. The following are samples of common internal polices used by private and public organizations. The reader's organization may have additional internal polices that must be considered when reaching a sourcing decision.

Many organizations, particularly those who are part of or who sell to federal, state or local governments, encourage purchasing from small business, minority-owned or other disadvantaged companies. In some cases, your customers may make it mandatory that some percentage of project dollars be given to facilities that meet the federal government's criteria. The Small Business Administration (SBA) in Washington, D.C., or local and regional offices can provide information on the criteria used to designate these groups and also help the buyer identify these types of sources. (See Appendices i and ii for federal government contacts. See Appendix iii for a partial listing of organizations that promote small and disadvantaged business interests.)

If a buyer is working for a division of a large private organization, he or she may be required to purchase from the parent company and/or its other divisions before going outside for alternate sources. In some cases, union contracts may require this approach, in others it may be a corporate policy. Some of the better run companies may require the buyer to get a quotation from the internal supplier, but leave the decision to purchase up to the buyer. If the internal source is not awarded the business, the buyer should be prepared to explain why and possibly provide feedback to the internal source. If the buyer provides one bidder with feedback, he or she should provide all bidders with the same information.

"Buy American" is another policy that can affect supplier selection. Many public and some private customers have included a "Buy American" clause in their contracts. Some percentage of the materials or materials and labor must be bought from United States firms. Other countries, notably Japan, have similar "buy domestic" requirements. With the advent of NAFTA and the need to be more competitive in the global marketplace, fewer customers are requiring domestic sourcing, thus allowing the buyer to find the best worldwide sources of supply.

"Buy locally" is similar to "Buy American" in that it encourages finding sources locally. It is different in that there may be economic or other reasons to buy locally. Response time for maintenance (ex: copiers) can be quicker with a local supplier. Top management's concerns for the organization's "image" may also require a buyer to look locally first, going out-of-town only if the goods or services are not available in-town.

All internal polices should be documented by a clear set of policy statements (corporate and purchasing). If the organization has relied on word-of-mouth, these policies need to be developed and put in place, defining "why," "how" and "when" a buyer should source from a given type of supplier.

Number of Suppliers

Many companies and organizations have decreased the number of suppliers they use on a regular basis. This has resulted in the commitment to buy a majority or all of the requirements for a particular part or like parts (ex: sheet metal) from a single supplier. There are advantages to sole sourcing and advantages to multiple sourcing. Which approach is best will depend upon what is being purchased, and in what quantity, upon the buyer's production processes, and upon the supplier marketplace. For example, it would be unusual to sole source lawn cutting/maintenance services for multiple plant locations in several states or countries.

Sole Sourcing

Usually a supplier will consider a buyer's business more favorably if it knows it is a sole source. High dollar/quantity purchases help even more. Many Just-In-Time (JIT) programs need sole sourcing to operate effectively. If the part or commodity is only available from one source (the supplier may hold critical patents or technologies, etc.), then the buyer has little choice (at least in the short run). Avoiding the payment of multiple, high tooling costs is another reason the buyer should consider sole sourcing. Sole sourcing should also be considered if the total quantities or dollar value is low. Whatever the reason for sole source, this does not necessarily mean the buyer is at the mercy of the supplier.

In exchange for sole sourcing, the buyer should expect to have more clout with the supplier. Generally speaking, the supplier should be more willing to give the buyer priority in times of market shortages and emergency buying situations. Better pricing should also be expected since the buyer is negotiating to buy larger quantities or spend more money than if he or she spread out the requirements to more than one supplier. Some purchasing operations have found it is easier to manage the supplier base and to reach and maintain quality levels if the buyer sole sources many parts or components. Lower administrative costs (time spent sourcing, processing purchase orders, expediting, etc.) can be expected since the buyer is dealing with fewer suppliers.

It is only common sense for the buyer to develop a supplier partnership with the sole source supplier in order to maximize the advantages of sole sourcing while minimizing the disadvantages.

Multiple Sourcing

Depending upon circumstances, multiple sourcing can be a better approach for a purchasing department. Having several suppliers or dividing up the business between two suppliers has several advantages. For example, disruptions in the smooth flow of supply due to shortages, labor unrest, wars or acts of God can sometimes be minimized by having several suppliers. In times of acute shortage, the buyer of sole sourced parts may be forced to look for alternative suppliers to avoid production line stoppages. Strikes or fires that impact one supplier's delivery seldom impact all suppliers. The buyer can also avoid being taken for granted or being taken advantage of by sole source suppliers if he or she uses multiple sources. Using several suppliers stimulates competition, helping to assure that suppliers don't get complacent. This is particularly important for buyers whose products have a short life cycle such as electronics where the buyer and his or her organization need to be constantly aware of new products and technological developments.

Most purchasing operations use a mixture of sole source and multiple source buying strategies to maximize competition while minimizing risk. Some organizations (notably the automotive industry) minimize their supplier base by dealing with suppliers who are responsible for many parts (ex: all brake parts). The supplier can deal with as many suppliers as it wants, but is a sole source contact for the buyer. This works well for parts for the automotive companies, but may not work well for other types of organizations.

Strategic Sourcing Agreements

Many forward looking organizations have developed or are developing Strategic Sourcing Alliances or Agreements (SSA). They have also been called Strategic Partnering or Supplier Partnership (though some lawyers advise against the terms "partner" or "partnership" since they have specific legal significance that implies joint liability to meet the obligations of the partners). There is a two-way exchange of information (financial, sales forecasts, technical, etc.) and expectations between each party. Over time, the parties develop a close relationship (some call it synergy) between buyer and seller where the success of both parties is tied together. Both parties help each other work toward meeting complementary goals or objectives.

There are several very good reasons to do this with key suppliers. They include maximizing leverage with suppliers and consolidating the supplier base for ease of supplier management. Other benefits can include shorter delivery or cycle times, more reliable delivery schedules, lower stocking levels at the buyer's operation, faster implementation of design changes and improved quality.

When should a buyer consider using SSA as a sourcing strategy? When the supplier or commodity is of key importance to the organization. Key importance can be defined as a critical item (ex: scrap for a steel-making operation), an item of a high dollar value, an item of a high yearly volume, an item in which a high degree of quality is required, or an item in which finding an alternate source of supply could be very expensive and time-consuming (due to high retooling costs, etc.).

How to establish an SSA process is beyond the scope of this book, but the basics are fairly straightforward. First, review all goods and services bought, identifying the key items and including opportunities for combining like requirements. Next, decide who will be on the team to develop the strategy (for departments, divisions, etc.) and obtain management support for the project.

Narrow the list of key items to the "A" items which can show the greatest return in the shortest time. Establish the goals and strategies to reach the goals. Implement the strategies and, lastly, review and measure the results.

Developing Strategic Supplier Alliances should be a continuous process rather than a one-time program. SSAs do not happen overnight. Trust, one of the major components of an SSA, takes time to develop. So does the research necessary to identify the key items, agree on the goals and develop the strategies necessary to reach the goals. While all these steps are time-consuming, the bottom line results are usually worthwhile. Buyers should consider using SSAs in their sourcing decision-making process.

Early Supplier Involvement Programs (ESI)

Early Supplier Involvement programs are exactly what the name implies — involving suppliers during the design phase. ESI can have a significantly positive impact on the bottom line if the suppliers are chosen carefully. The buyer can capitalize on the latest technologies, decrease design times and utilize supplier expertise to design a better and more competitive product. The potential cost savings and design improvements make ESI almost a must for high-volume manufactured parts.

Greater care must be taken in identifying sources for an ESI program. A supplier that can make good prototypes, but is not capable of supplying quality parts in the quantity needed for production should not be considered an ESI supplier. Needless to say, ESI suppliers should be considered supplier partners, nurtured and given special treatment such as fast pay, etc.

There are some disadvantages to using ESI. It will limit the number of suppliers on the front end, with the final selection almost always becoming sole source. Many suppliers wouldn't bother to make the effort unless they felt they would be rewarded with a order for most or all the requirements. The same arguments for and against sole sourcing apply here as well.

New vs. Current Suppliers

Purchasing often faces a paradox when it comes to deciding whether to source a part with current suppliers or look for new suppliers. Strategic Supplier Alliances and efforts to reduce the supplier base are steering purchasers toward using their current suppliers. The advantages of SSAs and a reduced supplier base have been noted above. Based on these strategies, a potential new supplier will have a difficult time getting an order.

The question arises: When should new suppliers be considered? First we need to classify the requirement as either recurring or new. If it is recurring, then the chances are that a supplier or suppliers already exist. If it is a requirement for a new item or service, then a supplier must be chosen.

Ordinarily, recurring requirements are given to suppliers that have provided the item in the past. The item's history file will show who the last supplier was and perhaps other sources as well. New suppliers should be considered when the buyer is concerned that the current supplier is taking advantage of the current situation. The supplier may be asking unreasonable prices and/or have quality, delivery or service problems. If the need is urgent, the current supplier cannot deliver in time, and the part is considered "off-the-shelf," then the buyer might also want to find a new supplier — at least temporarily. Another reason to look for a new supplier is the presence of major changes at the current supplier, such as a merger or changes in personnel, that can disrupt its operations.

New requirements give a buyer a chance to check the marketplace for new suppliers who may have new technologies and to assure competition. Note that new requirements of similar recurring parts can and often do go to current suppliers. In the final analysis, the buyer will have to decide if new suppliers can bring significant value to his or her organization. Price alone should not be the only reason to switch suppliers. Delivery, quality and service should also be considered.

Centralized vs. Decentralized Purchasing Operations

Academicians and business practitioners have spent countless hours discussing and arguing the issue of centralized versus decentralized organizational departments and structures. Each side has its own strengths and weaknesses which are well documented (ex: a centralized approach is more efficient; a decentralized approach is more responsive, etc.).

In theory, the faster pace of today's world economy would seem to support a more decentralized approach. Many large organizations are trying to recreate a small business climate in which decision-making is moved down to the lowest level possible to make the organization more nimble. "Empowerment" is one of the buzzwords that has become incorporated in Total Quality Management (TQM) programs. In addition to manufacturing operations, purchasing departments are subject to the trend as well. One Fortune 500 company expects each division or company to run its own purchasing operations without interference from "Corporate Purchasing." On the other hand, another large multi-division corporation is centralizing its purchasing operations. Both corporations are profitable as a whole. Each has weak, unprofitable divisions. What's going on here? What does the first company know that the second doesn't or vice versa?

From reading the literature available on centralized versus decentralized purchasing operations and discussing the subject with several purchasing professionals, it appears that the decision is not a clear-cut one. In fact, cutting through the biases, it appears to be situational. In other words, what works for Company A may not work for Company B. How then does this affect the sourcing decision?

In a centralized purchasing operation, many goods and services are placed on organization-wide contracts lasting a year or more. During this time, all purchases of a particular part or group of parts are expected to be awarded to the approved/contracted supplier. The same arguments of sole sourcing vs. multiple sourcing apply here as well.

Conclusion

Decision-making, when identifying and choosing sources of supply, will depend upon the internal environment, policies and procedures of the organization. Well-run purchasing departments will quantify these factors in a written Policy & Procedures Manual. This manual should be given to everyone with purchasing authority and made available to all suppliers and potential suppliers.

A note of caution needs to be raised at this point. This chapter has raised several internal considerations that can affect the sourcing decision. The buyer may be tempted to check what the current situation is in his or her organization and accept it without comment. This may be a mistake. In the dynamic ever-changing world economy, purchasing strategies, policies and procedures that worked in the past may not work in the future. A world-class purchasing organization will review itself and make adjustments in how it goes about sourcing the goods and services it buys. If it doesn't, the organization's ability to compete can be jeopardized.

EXTERNAL
CONSIDERATIONS
AND **T**HEIR **I**MPACT ON
SOURCING **D**ECISION

CHAPTER **3**

The previous chapter reviewed internal factors related to sourcing. This chapter will discuss the external factors. Specifically it will address market conditions; buying from manufacturers directly or through distribution; the pros and cons of buying locally, nationally, and globally; social, political and environmental considerations; and legal considerations that impact the sourcing decision-making process.

Marketplace Conditions

Classical economic theory states that there are three types of marketplace conditions — pure competition (many sellers), monopoly (one seller), and imperfect competition (a few sellers or many sellers of differentiated products). In theory, it would seem that buyers would prefer to have many possible suppliers since competition promotes best cost situations (cost, delivery, quality,

---

GLOBAL **S**OURCING   **21**

service and technology). Realistically, the most money is spent in imperfect competition or, in sole source situations — monopolistic marketplaces. This is particularly true for complex or high technology parts that require investment of significant amounts of money and equipment to get started.

Sourcing in a Pure Competition Marketplace

A pure competition marketplace has many buyers and sellers. All players are generally equal in their market share — that is to say no one buyer or seller dominates the market. The products are not differentiated. This means that one seller's product is not more desirable than any other's product. Buyers and sellers are free to enter and leave the market at anytime. This condition usually means that investments in capital or equipment are minimal to enter the marketplace. Supply and demand alone determine the prices. It is also assumed that both buyers and sellers will try to maximize their advantage by acting is a reasonable and rational manner (i.e., to minimize cost and maximize profit).

One example of pure competition might be a farmer's market where fruits and vegetables are bought and sold. Each purchase is subject to negotiation with wild swings in prices possible. The market is almost always unstable with buyers and sellers entering or leaving constantly. Most purchasers prefer to buy products that have a more predictable and stable pricing and supply structure. For these reasons, pure competition exists more often in theory than in reality.

Sourcing in a Monopolistic Marketplace

In a monopoly, one seller controls all of the supply of a particular product. Since the seller controls the availability, that supplier also controls the price and will act to maximize its profit by regulating supply. To avoid unfair market prices, most monopolies such as utilities are regulated. One monopoly that has survived for decades relatively unregulated is the distribution of diamonds by the De Beers organization. Even this is being challenged by suppliers of diamonds from Russia and other countries.

Sourcing in Imperfect Competition

Whether the market consists of a few sellers (oligopoly) or many sellers of differentiated products, most buying and selling takes place under conditions of imperfect competition. Generally speaking, the marketplace is still competitive. Buyers of gasoline find the market varies from highly competitive to almost collusive. Gasoline sellers strive to increase the price during the summer peak driving months when the volume of gasoline demand increases. While prices may appear to increase in lockstep, in reality market forces of supply and demand are at work. Prices fall again in the non-peak seasons. Prices will also fall if one or more suppliers decides to try to increase its market share. It is up to the buyer to find the best price for gasoline at any given time.

U.S. Congressional and Justice Department investigations do find a few conspiracies to fix prices, but by and large there is competition taking place, though perhaps indirectly. For example, suppliers may appear to be noncompetitive, keeping prices firm for long periods of time, but they may offer additional services such as keeping inventory on hand, giving special payment terms or other value-added services that generate indirect price reductions.

When there are many sellers of differentiated products, competition is more apparent. Many consumer and industrial products fall under this classification. In this type of marketplace, a seller may spend a lot of time and money trying to make the buyer believe that his or her product is better than the other sellers' products. For example, aspirin is aspirin, whether brand name or generic. However, drug companies spend millions of dollars on advertising to get the buyer to buy their product ("Our quality is better," "We cost less," etc.). It is the buyer's responsibility to weigh price, quality, delivery and service information to find the best cost supplier and negotiate the best deal for his or her organization.

Buying From Manufacturers Directly Or Through Distribution

Many times a buyer is faced with a choice of dealing directly with a manufacturer or buying from a distributor of the manufacturer's products. Sometimes, particularly if the volume of business is low, a manufacturer will require the purchaser to buy through distribution. There are advantages to both approaches and a wise buyer may want to negotiate a way to purchase products from both sources.

Manufacturer Direct
or Original Equipment Manufacturer (OEM) Buying

Dealing directly with a manufacturer can save a buyer money since there are no middle parties that charge a fee for their services. Technical questions, quality and delivery issues can be addressed directly between the buyer and the seller instead of being relayed through a third party. Depending upon the F.O.B. point and routing, transportation costs can also be less. With these advantages in mind, many buyers prefer to deal directly with the manufacturer for large dollar or large volume buys. This is particularly true if the product is custom or semi-custom made for the buyer.

Conversely, manufacturers of standard commodities and products historically have not been willing to handle small orders. They may require a minimum quantity or a minimum dollar value for each item. The reason is simple economies of scale. From the selling expense point of view, a salesperson can spend an hour making a $1,000 sale or a $1,000,000 sale. The amount of effort is the same, but the impact to the bottom line is greater with a larger sale. Furthermore, bulk packaging is cheaper than individual packaging. Truck load shipments are cheaper than less-than-truck load shipments. Manufacturers don't want to take the financial risk of extending credit to everyone. Also, the manufacturer's Accounts Receivable costs are less as a percentage of the total invoice value. The buyer will have to negotiate with the manufacturer, perhaps offering to do more business, to obtain favorable OEM buys.

Buying From Distribution

There are advantages to buying from distribution. For example, distributors purchase in large quantities and sell in smaller quantities. This permits buyers of small quantities to avoid large minimum orders from a manufacturer. Distributors also typically offer the buyer some additional value or service. The value or service can be carrying inventory for immediate shipment, additional processing (ex: cutting material to the buyer's specifications), favorable payment terms, technical assistance, or other such services. The distributor makes its profit by marking up the price of the material and by charging for its services. The added cost may still be less than if the buyer had to provide its own services.

Typically distributors carry more than one product or brand. This is advantageous to the buyer in two ways. First, when more

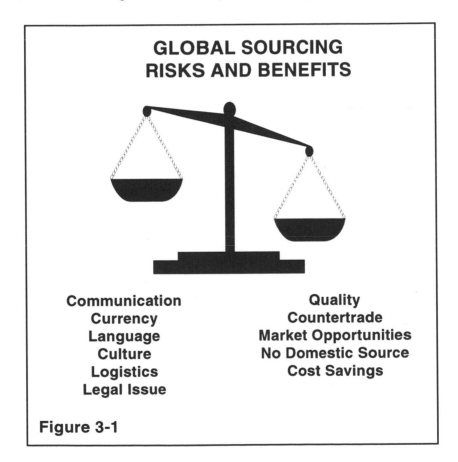

GLOBAL SOURCING RISKS AND BENEFITS

Communication	**Quality**
Currency	**Countertrade**
Language	**Market Opportunities**
Culture	**No Domestic Source**
Logistics	**Cost Savings**
Legal Issue	

Figure 3-1

than one brand is available, there is competition. Second, with multiple products available, the buyer can place one order for several parts instead of placing multiple orders with several manufacturers. This saves purchasing process time and overhead costs. This cost saving is one reason why some MRO buyers are implementing systems contracting with distributors.

Whichever method works better will vary depending upon the commodity being bought, the quantity, and the buyer's need for additional services. Considering price, quality, delivery and service, the bottom line question to ask is: "Which approach gives my organization the best buy?"

Buying From Local Or National Suppliers

All other considerations being equal, most buyers prefer to purchase from local suppliers. The operative word is "equal." Many buyers equate short distance with better service, quicker and more accurate deliveries (especially in a Just-In-Time environment), lower transportation charges and shorter lead-times which can mean lower inventory levels. It is true that the longer the supply chain, the more time it takes to get something from point A to point B. Also, statistically there is a greater chance of something happening to interrupt or delay the smooth flow of goods over longer distances. Dealing with local suppliers also meets what Dobler and Lee call "implied social responsibilities to the community."[1] Many organizations have purchasing policies that favor local suppliers for these reasons.

Buying from national suppliers does offer some advantages over local suppliers. First of all, not all goods and services are available locally. This is particularly true if the buyer's plant is located in a rural area. Second, due to larger production capacities and larger stocking programs, national suppliers may be able to handle changes in demand better than local suppliers. If the national supplier is larger than the local supplier (which is often the case), technical assistance may be more readily available to the buyer.

Buying From Global/International Suppliers

Significant Trade Agreements

GATT

GATT stands for "General Agreement on Tariffs and Trade." GATT has been renegotiated seven times since the original agreement in 1948. In 1994, after many years of negotiation, the U.S. and 122 other countries have signed a new GATT agreement (called the Uruguay Round) whose intent is to create a predictable international trading field in which to transact business. The new agreement took effect on July 1, 1995, with some provisions taking effect immediately and others being phased in over ten years. Tariffs on thousands of manufactured items ranging from beer to high-tech electronics are being significantly reduced. For the first time, service industries have been included as well. Intellectual property rights (patents, copyrights, etc.) are now protected worldwide. The GATT administration system has been replaced with the World Trade Organization (WTO). The WTO will not only administer the agreement, but will provide a forum for resolving disputes between and among countries.

From a purchasing standpoint, it is too early to tell whether this latest round will be beneficial to all or to select industries (particularly since some provisions will not be implemented until 2005). In theory, new sources of supply will become available to the buyer, creating new competition which will improve product innovation, quality, delivery and customer satisfaction. Increased predictability of international marketplaces is also a plus. Buyers currently using domestic suppliers may find it advantageous to source overseas, particularly if their domestic sources go out of business due to foreign competition.

NAFTA

The North American Free Trade Agreement (NAFTA) was approved by the U.S. in November 1993. Unlike GATT, NAFTA currently has only three countries that have signed the agreement (Canada, Mexico, and the United States). Other countries in the

Americas have expressed interest in joining (particularly Chile), but it is too early to tell if NAFTA will be come AFTA. According to the Organization of American States:

> Article 102 sets out the objectives of the three countries in entering into the NAFTA. The Article contains: a statement that the Agreement is based on the fundamental principles of national treatment, most-favoured-nation (MFN) treatment, and transparency; a commitment to facilitate the cross-border movement of goods and services; a commitment to provide adequate and effective protection and enforcement of intellectual property rights; a statement calling for effective domestic procedures for the implementation and application of the Agreement; and a rule of interpretation requiring the Parties to apply the Agreement in the light of its objectives and in accordance with international law.[2]

Like GATT, NAFTA is time-phased with tariffs decreasing through the year 2004. NAFTA also covers service industries. Depending upon whom you ask, NAFTA is an opportunity or an albatross. Many purchasers find doing business with Canada is easier after the "Rules of Origin" regulations have been deciphered. Business with Mexico has been more of a mixed bag. Some companies assemble products in Mexico with relative ease while others are struggling. Also, transportation agreements have been put on hold that would have permitted Canadian, Mexican and U.S. truckers to pass through the Mexico/U.S. boarder without having to unload their cargoes. This plus infrastructure (roads, etc.) challenges make it harder to do business with Mexico. Recent devaluation of the Mexican peso has also contributed to negative press in the United States about NAFTA. In addition, labor unions and others have raised concerns about losing jobs due to NAFTA. If the buyer's organization is unionized, it may not be advantageous to pursue sourcing opportunities under NAFTA if it will cause labor problems. Each organization will have to research and decide if NAFTA will work for its requirements.

The U.S. Commerce Department is a good starting point for finding out more information on GATT and NAFTA and how these agreements might affect the buyer's organization. Other organizations or divisions of the buyer's organization that are currently utilizing GATT and/or NAFTA are also good sources of information.

Advantages to Buying Internationally

Research by purchasing academics has tended to identify cost as the main reason for going overseas. Oliver Williamson suggests that international sourcing is a way to lower organizational transaction costs.[3] Day and Wensley claim that an organization is trying to develop a competitive advantage by sourcing internationally.[4] Monczka and Giunipero note several advantages to sourcing internationally. They include: 1) cost/price; 2) increased competition; 3) assuring supply; 4) obtaining technology; 5) higher quality; 6) access to new markets; and 7) make/buy alternatives.[5] Dobler and Burt split out Monczka and Giunipero's third advantage into timeliness of delivery and broadening the supply base, and add countertrade.[6]

The heavy emphasis once placed on cost savings may be now be shifting. There is one study of international sourcing by Sharland and Giunipero that was presented at the 1994 International Purchasing Conference in Atlanta that concluded that "the most important relationship found in this study was that between quality in the finished goods market and the sourcing arrangements (time period and negotiation process)."[7]

Recent discussions by the author with several international buyers also seem to indicate that purchasing managers and practitioners may not emphasize cost savings as much as before. A Fortune 500 company in the electrical appliance industry uses a benchmark of 25% cost savings from an overseas supplier versus a domestic supplier before it will consider buying internationally. A major computer maker uses 20%. Several manufacturing organizations have actually returned to domestic sources of supply. Quality, lack of domestic sources, new market access and countertrade were the main reasons mentioned by this group.

Disadvantages and Risks of Buying Internationally

There are several disadvantages and risks associated with purchasing overseas that the buyer must consider. Perhaps the most often cited disadvantage is communication. Language, customs and culture can create barriers that can make buying overseas a real challenge. For example "Hai" in Japanese means, "Yes." It also means, "Yes, I hear you." Japanese consider it impolite to say "No." Many international buyers believing that an agreement had been reached were surprised to find out later that what they had understood was not what the foreign supplier understood.

In addition, Western ethics are not the same as Eastern ethics. For example, reciprocity is considered an integral part of doing business in Japan, while in the United States it may considered unethical or even illegal. In another example, a consultant negotiating with an Asian firm for an American company was asked to join the foreign firm midway through the process. While it may seem grossly unethical to Westerners, many Asian suppliers would find nothing wrong with this approach.

Cultural differences can also lead to misunderstandings. People in the United States view individualism as very important and reward individual effort accordingly. On the other hand, the Japanese citizen is instilled from early childhood with the belief that the group or team is more important than the individual. This is one reason why decision-making takes longer in Japan — all parties must reach agreement. United States buyers unfamiliar with Japanese culture complain that a simple yes or no question takes forever to get answered.

Currency issues are another risk that international buyers must consider. It is a well-known fact that currency exchange rates can fluctuate widely (in some cases within minutes). This can lead to unstable pricing. For example, a contract agreed upon today with payment on delivery (a common payment term) six months from now may negatively impact either party's bottom line. Assume for purposes of this exercise that a United States buyer has agreed to pay a Mexican firm $1,000,000 in Mexican pesos. When the agreement was reached the dollar to peso exchange rate was 1 to 1. A major devaluation of the peso decreases the ratio to 1 to 2. The U.S. buyer's cost is now $500,000 — a tremendous cost reduction! However if the dollar decreases in value, the U.S. buyer's costs go up accordingly. Attempting to manage this risk by hedging foreign currencies is not recommended for the uninitiated or inexperienced buyer. Learning curves are steep, and it is a "no prisoners" environment in the foreign currency exchanges markets. Several years ago a major computer company had to write off several million dollars, turning a profitable year into a loss, due to losses from trying to hedge dollars to yen in the foreign currency exchange market.

Logistics are another concern faced by the international buyer. In some cases, product must cross oceans to get from supplier to buyer. This increases the front end lead-time. The longer the supply chain, the greater chance a disruption can occur, such as storms at sea, dock worker strikes, etc. In other cases such as Mexico, not all roads are four-lane, divided highways. Some roads between the supplier and the buyer may be unpaved. A U.S. buyer, used to his or her Interstate road system, may expect quicker delivery than is possible. To avoid stockout situations created by logistics, higher levels of inventory may have to be kept on hand. Transportation costs are also increased.

Customs forms, certificates of origin, inspection certificates and other documentation are required to get products from one country to another. A whole industry of consultants and organizations has developed to help the buyer and supplier. This adds additional costs that in some cases cannot or should not be avoided. Customs duties and trade wars can also add additional risks and costs to an international buy.

Legal issues, particularly when a dispute cannot be negotiated between the parties, can also create challenges for the international buyer. There is an international court in The Hague in the Netherlands, but most organizations prefer that, for cost, language, own turf situations, and other reasons, cases should be argued in their own country. Given this preference, the question arises, "Which country's court system will try the case?" This can be particularly important since a country's laws can favor one side over the other. For example, as of this writing, copyright laws and their enforcement are much tougher in the United States than in China. A supplier of software would obviously prefer to have a copyright infringement case tried in the U.S.

There are also physical risks to personnel associated with buying overseas. The U.S. State Department publishes travel advisories for international travelers. Several private security or risk consultants also provide this kind of information, as well as information on political stability and other risks associated with doing business in a specific country.

In the final analysis, there are risks and benefits associated with international sourcing. An organization must carefully review all available information before it can decide whether or not it is worthwhile to enter the international sourcing arena. Many forward-looking organizations use a team approach to deciding whether to source overseas. In addition to purchasing, people from engineering, marketing/sales, accounting, accounting and top management or some combination of departments may help make the decision. These organizations generally expect the buyer to provide leadership to the team whose job it is to quantify as much as possible all factors involved in making the decision.

Social, Political And Environmental Considerations

Few bid systems make allowance for these "soft" or unquantifiable issues. Many buyers do not weigh social, political or environmental considerations heavily, unless their customers (internal or external) demand it. For example, top management of a major fast food chain decided to change its product packaging from Styrofoam to recycled (and recyclable) paper. The company wanted to create a real "green" image, believing correctly that it would be viewed more favorably by its customers. Styrofoam packaging suppliers had to be replaced quickly with new suppliers capable of providing recycled paper products with the additional ability (in some cases) to buy back the organization's paper waste for further recycling.

In another case, a major discount retailer was criticized for buying product from clothing suppliers who used sweatshops or exploited workers in countries that had weak or unenforced labor laws. Labor unions and politicians started a nationwide boycott, forcing the retailer to buy from "labor friendly" suppliers. "Buy

American" is another example of how these soft issues must be taken into account.

Generally speaking, buyers have been reactive to these kinds of issues, in part because their customers (internal and/or external) perceived price or other buying criteria to be more important. Purchasing needs to be sensitive to the social, political and environmental issues that can affect its organization and make allowances for them. This can be as simple as identifying and using environmentally friendly suppliers or as complex as adding additional criteria to their bid evaluation systems. If the buyer's management or the organization's customers expect a certain image, purchasing must be prepared to identify and buy from suppliers that support this image.

Legal Issues

Laws that govern business transactions and contracts vary. In the United States, the state of Louisiana bases its commercial laws on the Napoleonic Code. The remaining states use British Common Law codified by the Uniform Commercial Code. As noted above, laws can and do vary also from country to country. Buyers should have a basic understanding of contract law for each country or state in which they are or will be doing business.

In the U.S., the buyer should understand how the Uniform Commercial Code, the Clayton Act and the Robinson-Patman Act affects his or her dealings with suppliers. A good reference book that explains legal aspects of the purchasing job is the *Purchasing Manager's Desk Book of Purchasing Law* by James J. Ritterskamp, Jr. and Donald D. King.[8]

When a buyer sources outside the U.S., he or she should reach agreement with the supplier as to which country's laws will govern the transactions. In the early 1980s, the United Nations developed the "United Nation's Convention on Contracts for the International Sale of Goods," otherwise known as the "CISG." It covers sales of goods between businesses in different countries. However, it does not apply to sales of services or consumer purchases. It should also be noted that not all countries have adopted the CISG and therefore it may not be applicable in all circumstances.

The good news for U.S. buyers is that the UCC and CISG are very similar for the most part. However, there are several significant differences. For example, under the UCC, an acceptance of an offer can have different terms than the original offer. The Knock Out Rule applies to decide if a contract exists. On the other hand, contracts under the CISG must have exactly the same terms in the offer and the acceptance. In addition, the CISG accepts oral contracts as valid and enforceable while the UCC requires contracts over $500 to be in writing to be enforceable. These and other differences make it imperative that a buyer have a good understanding of the CISG before agreeing to a contract that will be governed by its clauses.

Generally speaking, suppliers want to have the laws of the country or state where they are located to apply to any contracts or purchase orders. As noted above, it is to the buyer's advantage to negotiate legal venue to his or her location. When in doubt, the buyer should consult with corporate or private attorneys. A buyer's ignorance of legal issues affecting a contract is not an acceptable excuse when legal problems arise.

Conclusion

The external conditions or factors mentioned above can all impact a buyer's sourcing decision either positively or negatively. It would be unusual for all the external factors to affect the sourcing exercise. Furthermore, some factors may have a greater or lesser impact than others depending upon what commodity or service is being bought and when it is being bought. There may also be other external factors not mentioned that are specific to the buyer's industry or service that may also affect the sourcing decision. It is also worth noting that the external factors can be as dynamic as internal factors. Therefore the buyer should be constantly aware of external changes that can affect his or her sourcing decisions.

---

[1]   *Purchasing and Supply Management, 6th. ed.*, Donald Dobler and Burt Lee, McGraw-Hill, 1996.

[2] *OAS Overview of the North American Free Trade Agreement*, Chapter 1, http://www.nafta.net/naftagre.htm.

[3] *The Economic Institutions of Capitalism*, Oliver Williamson, Boston Free Press, 1985.

[4] "Marketing Theory with a Strategic Orientation," George Day and Robin Wensley, *Journal of Marketing*, vol. 47, Fall 1983.

[5] *Purchasing Internationally*, Robert Monczka and Larry Giunipero, Chelsea, MI, Bookcrafters, 1990.

[6] *Purchasing and Supply Management*, 6th. ed., Donald Dobler and Burt Lee, McGraw-Hill, 1996.

[7] "International Outsourcing: A Current Analysis," Alex Sharland and Larry Giunipero, C.P.M., *N.A.P.M. 79th Annual International Purchasing Conference Proceedings*, N.A.P.M., Tempe, AZ, 1994.

[8] *Purchasing Manager's Desk Book of Purchasing Law*, 2nd edition, by James J. Ritterskamp, Jr. and Donald D. King (Prentice Hall, 1993).

IDENTIFYING SOURCES OF SUPPLY

CHAPTER FOUR

After the buyer has found out what is needed and considered the internal and external conditions that will affect sourcing, he or she needs to find and identify potential sources of supply. Being able to locate suppliers capable of meeting the organization's requirements is one of the more significant responsibilities of purchasing.

Buying goods or services that have been purchased before may be as easy as checking the purchasing history files for approved suppliers. Unless there is an overpowering reason not to use previous suppliers, the job of finding a source is over. However, not all purchases are repetitive. Also the buyer may not want to use past suppliers for a number of reasons (poor quality, late delivery, etc.). So where does a buyer look for qualified suppliers?

Buyers have many places available and services willing to help them find suppliers. The methodologies for finding domestic and overseas sources of supply is similar in some aspects, but they are different enough to warrant treating each separately.

Domestic Sources Of Supply

In some respects, finding domestic sources of supply is easier and less costly than finding overseas suppliers. That said, where does a buyer go to find these suppliers? Similar to conditions affecting the sourcing decision, there are internal and external resources that the buyer can use.

In-house and Existing Suppliers

One sourcing resource many buyers use is their own in-house supplier cards or supplier data files. The more sophisticated systems (paper or computerized) provide information on types of products offered by the supplier, brand names, etc. as well as the supplier's name, address, phone number and contact person. An approved supplier file for repeat buys is another immediate source of supplier information. Both of these sources should always be checked first since they can provide a history of suppliers' pricing, quality and delivery performance.

Other buyers who may have purchased the commodity or service in the past are another good internal source of information. Engineers and drafting personnel may be able to assist a buyer in finding a supplier (particularly if the supplier was designed in). In one case, a vice president of Sales helped find a specialized electrical cabinet supplier by asking his customers which suppliers they used. If the buyer works for a large organization, corporate purchasing or buyers in other divisions can also be helpful in identifying potential suppliers.

Existing supplier's salespeople and supplier catalogs are another place to find information. If you already buy one type of screw from a supplier, it may be able to supply you with other types of screws. The information may only be a telephone call away. In addition, since you are already dealing with the supplier, supplier performance is known and a line of credit information doesn't have to be redone.

Outside/New Places for Sourcing Information

So far we have looked in-house and at existing suppliers for sourcing information. If these places cannot provide a sufficient of potential suppliers, the buyer has other options.

The telephone book (White and/or Yellow pages) is an inexpensive place to find suppliers. So are trade directories, registers, magazines and journals (ex: *Purchasing* magazine has many supplier advertisements in it and is free to qualified buyers). Trade shows and supplier fairs/exhibits are another good way to locate suppliers. All buyers who have been purchasing for a length of time receive solicited or unsolicited mailings (sometimes called "Bingo Cards") from potential suppliers advertising their products. The Internet, another good source of supplier information will be covered in another chapter. The U.S. Department of Commerce and the Small Business Administration are also good places to find suppliers, particularly if a buyer is looking for small or disadvantaged suppliers (see Appendix ii).

Overseas Sources Of Supply

Finding suppliers overseas can be challenging. Before looking for international suppliers, the buyer should ask him or herself (or the buying team), "Is the part or assembly a likely candidate for international sourcing?" One method of determining this was developed by Raul Casillas of Alps Manufacturing, a suplier to Apple Computers in the disk drive area. The following questions must all be answered "yes" if international sourcing can be considered a real possibility:

1) **Does it qualify as "high-volume" in your industry?**
2) **Does it have a long life (two to three years)?**
3) **Does it lend itself to repetitive manufacturing or assembly?**
4) **Is demand for the product fairly stable?**
5) **Are specifications and drawings clear and well defined?**

6) **Is technology not available domestically at a competitive price and quality?**[1]

Dale Reynolds of Digital Appliance Controls, a division of Emerson Electric, further defines "high-volume" as a minimum of tens of thousands of parts. In addition, he makes a strong case for making sure the design is fairly stable and not subject to many engineering or design specification changes. Both Casillas and Reynolds also cite commitment from top management and a willingness of the organization to take as long term an approach as necessary for a successful international sourcing exercise.

Okay, your organization has decided to try to source internationally. Now what? How does a buyer get started locating and qualifying foreign sources?

The easiest way to get started is to check with other purchasers in the buyer's organization. They might be located at the buyer's plant, in another sister division, or perhaps at the corporate headquarters. If the buyer's company is already using one or more acceptable foreign suppliers, the buyer may be able to save time and effort by piggybacking onto existing agreements or at least using the existing supplier channels.

Intermediaries

Perhaps the next easiest way to get started is by using existing "middle men" or intermediaries. There are several different types of intermediaries, each offering different services with costs ranging from free to a percentage of the total sale. Generally speaking, the more complex and numerous the services employed, the greater the fee charged. A prudent buyer will identify what kinds of service he or she needs and not pay for extra services. Intermediaries can be located through several sources including N.A.P.M. national and affiliate offices, trade organizations, trade journals, transportation companies and the Department of Commerce.

Import Merchants

If the buyer's product is a standard commodity such as cloth, then an import merchant who buys and sells cloth for its own profit may be simplest way to go. Import merchants handle all logistical details (customs, currency exchange, transportation, etc.). For all intents and purposes, the buyer can handle the purchase like any other domestic purchase.

Subsidiaries of Foreign Companies

Balance of trade pressures and other forces have led some foreign companies to set up subsidiaries in the United States. Depending upon the subsidiary, the services can range from language translation to the same services offered by import merchants. Costs can range from zero to 33% for these services. The buyer should be warned that the subsidiary is an additional link in the supply chain and usually does not have direct contact with the supplier's manufacturing operations. This can create problems when the buyer needs to expedite, change an order or change a specification quickly. Answers can take weeks to obtain instead of days.

Trading Companies

Trading companies operate like import merchants on a worldwide scale and have existed for several hundred years. The British and other colonial powers used trading companies to trade with China and other countries in the Pacific Rim. Perhaps one of the better known was the East India Company. A number of trading companies based in Hong Kong can trace their roots back several centuries. A buyer can easily find directories and listings of these kinds of firms and their scope of services in trade journals and newspapers such as the *Wall Street Journal*.

Commission Houses

Commission houses are usually agents for foreign exporters and are paid by the exporters on a commission basis for what they sell. Generally speaking they do not buy the goods themselves, but do handle customs and shipping details.

Agents

Agents are organizations or individuals who represent foreign sellers. They are paid on a commission basis. Similar to domestic real estate agents, their loyalty and responsibility is to the seller. They do not take title of the goods or handle any financial responsibility and are simply a conduit handling the customs and shipping details only.

Import Brokers

International import brokers bring buyers and sellers together. An import broker's commission is paid by the seller if it locates buyers and by the buyer if it finds sources of supply. Import brokers do not handle any financial or logistical details. If the buyer has limited or no experience sourcing overseas and is not sure it is worthwhile, import brokers may be the best approach.

International Procurement Offices (IPO)

Larger firms doing millions of dollars of business in a country or particular region might want to set up their own purchasing or procurement offices. Opinion varies as to the minimum dollar value, but most experts agree it must be over $20 million per year. It should be noted that contract IPOs do exist. They are willing to provide service to multiple companies whose dollar volumes make setting up their own IPO infeasible. Using a contract IPO reduces some of the cost associated with setting up your own IPO, but some buyers have concerns about loyalty and service.

IPOs can provide on-site evaluation of suppliers, including pricing, delivery, quality and service issues. They can also provide an "ear-to-the-ground" concerning a foreign country's political, economic and social climates as well as labor issues that could affect the supplier's ability to provide goods and services.

A typical IPO is staffed partially or completely with the foreign country's nationals or perhaps by expatriates. In some cases, nationals from the buyer's firm may provide a supervisory or staffing role as well. The IPO is often treated as a separate cost center by the parent organization, making its revenue by charging a small percentage (usually 1% to 5%) for its services.

Direct Or OEM Purchasing From Foreign Suppliers

Avoiding the intermediary or IPO and dealing directly with a foreign supplier usually nets the buyer the lowest delivered cost (including customs duties, transportation, etc.). However it may not be the lowest total cost when travel, communication and other costs are factored into the calculation. A note of caution needs to be injected at this time. Many expert international buyers recommend that the organization purchase the commodities or products needed through intermediaries first to develop an understanding of the market conditions, the social, political and economic trends, of the target country before considering buying from overseas OEMs. Generally speaking, most buyers should not deal directly with a foreign supplier until they have developed a "warm and fuzzy" feeling concerning the supplier's ability to deliver a competitive and quality product on time. The buyer must do a careful analysis (cost/benefit, etc.) before deciding to deal directly with the foreign supplier. The type of analysis used to decide whether to use a domestic OEM supplier or distribution channels applies here as well.

Identifying Foreign OEM Suppliers

Finding foreign OEM suppliers is similar to finding domestic suppliers — it just may require more inquiries and time. There are several approaches to finding overseas suppliers.

If the buyer is in a countertrade situation, his or her marketing people may be able to get supplier names from the customer. In some cases, the customer may dictate which supplier(s) will do business with the buyer's company. Finding suppliers by this method is relatively quick and effortless, but the buyer may run the standard risks associated with a noncompetitive supplier base.

Another approach is to contact the embassy or trade office of the country or countries with whom the buyer is interested in doing business. (See Appendix iv for a listing of embassies in the U.S.) It can be time-consuming trying to decipher an embassy telephone directory since some embassies call their contact person a commercial attaché or other similar bureaucratic title that may not clearly describe the person the buyer needs to reach. When contacting an embassy, one successful approach has been to phrase the request something like this: "I'm interested in buying XYZ products (or commodities) from your country. Who can I talk with to find out the names of several potential suppliers?" Embassies also have World Wide Web (WWW) sites that can also provide preliminary contact information. Sources provided by embassy personnel may or may not have been "vetted" or checked out by the host country as viable suppliers, so buyer beware and do your homework. With this approach, the buyer will probably have to make several more contacts to obtain enough information to locate potential suppliers.

Some international buyers use trade associations or trade journals to find foreign OEM suppliers. (See Appendix v for information and directories dealing with the European Union. See Appendix vi for a partial listing of Pacific Rim Electronics directories.) Another approach is to contact the N.A.P.M. and ask for information on international sourcing. N.A.P.M. also has International committees at national, district and affiliate levels that can provide a buyer an information network to help identify foreign suppliers. International trade shows or fairs are another place to pick up information.

Conclusion

Identifying potential sources of supply is one of the most important aspects of a buyer's job. Developing an information network of domestic and international suppliers is an ongoing job. Some savvy buyers keep an index of contacts and sources and use it to find additional suppliers. This way they can make sure that they are getting the "best buy" from their supplier base.

---

[1]   "Foreign Sourcing: Is it For You?," Raul Casillas, *Pacific Purchaser*, November/December 1988, p. 9.

SOURCING
ON THE
INTERNET

CHAPTER FIVE

This chapter will provide the buyer with some background and basics about the Internet and how it relates to sourcing. The Internet offers a wealth of opportunities and some risks for the buyer. Most buyers will probably be using the Internet to source and purchase goods and services before the year 2000.

Internet Background

What Is The Internet And Why Is It Important To A Buyer?

The Internet is a world-wide collection of tens of thousands of computer networks which tie together over twenty million computers in over 100 countries around the world. The Internet has doubled in size every year since 1988. Originally designed to create an information exchange link between educational institutions and government facilities, it has exploded into an "information superhighway" that provides communication and information to anyone who has the computer software and hardware (an "on-ramp") to access it. The buying and selling of goods and services is taking place on it daily. Many organizations use it to communicate what they offer for sale and how to get in touch with them. These World Wide Web (WWW or Web) pages offer the buyer a wealth of sourcing information on an international scale.

Electronic Data Interchange (EDI) will be able to be accomplished with almost any supplier. "Currently only 5% of companies use EDI because of the expensive private-network infrastructure. As a low-cost conduit. . . the Internet promises to open up EDI for use by millions of businesses."[1] Several suppliers are marketing Internet services to connect buyers and sellers claiming to offer secure RFQ and bid award conduit. See Appendix viii for a partial listing.

Information sharing (e-mail, specifications, drawings, etc.) between geographically separated departments and divisions or between buyer and supplier is becoming a standard practice. It is the wave of the future as far as business and commercial activity is concerned. Wise buyers will learn how to use the Internet to help them do their jobs more efficiently and effectively.

How Does A Buyer Connect To The Internet?

The buyer will need a computer with enough memory to support the application, a modem (14.4 kbaud or above is recommended), a telephone line, and software to connect the computer to an Internet provider. The hardware can be obtained from many sources if the buyer's organization doesn't already have it in place. Internet software can be found in any software store for around $50.00. It is also possible to get Internet software free. Like computers, there are many versions of software that will connect a user to the Internet. Netscape Navigator, Microsoft Explorer, and Spry Internet in a Box are three products that have the greatest market share currently. All three do a good job of connecting the user to the "net." The buyer should consult his or her organization's Information Systems department for guidance to establish and maintain consistent software and hardware standards.

Once the hardware and software are installed, an Internet provider is needed to hook up to the "net." The access supplier will provide a "host address" (connection information) that is needed by the Internet software to make a connection to the Internet. Almost all higher education institutions are on the "net" and some offer accounts to the public (though there may be some restrictions). There are independent providers as well, ranging from America Online and CompuServe to local and regional suppliers. Local and long distance telephone companies also offer access in some areas. Currently, monthly rates per user range from $10.00 for six hours of Internet access to $30.00 for unlimited access. Additionally, for those who travel internationally, AOL, for a small hourly rate, offers local numbers in each country to allow you to connect worldwide.

The buyer, with help from other departments, should use good purchasing techniques to find the best source for his or her organization's needs. Note that other departments such as Sales may want to be connected as well, so a "full service" provider who can help create and support a Web page for Sales as well as provide access may be necessary.

Internet Basics

There are literally hundreds of books that offer advice on how to use the Internet. Unfortunately, they are usually overtaken by events (OBE) and become obsolete before they are printed. There are some basics that are consistent however.

To access another organization, the buyer needs to knows the Internet address or "URL." For an organization, this address consists of a header (usually "http://www."), a host (a computer name) with the rightmost part stating the "domain" where it belongs. Note that most addresses are lower case and must be entered exactly as written. The main domains are:

COM   **Commercial Organizations**
            (ex: Ford Motor Co. — http://www.ford.com)

EDU   **Education/Academic Organizations**
            (ex: Harvard — http://www.harvard.edu)

GOV   **Government**
             (ex: The White House
                   http://www.whitehouse.gov)

NET   **Networks or organizations running networks**
             (ex: Industry Net — http://www.industry.net)

ORG   **Organizations that don't fit other classifications**
             (ex: N.A.P.M. — http://www.napm.org)

As another example, Pro-Tech's Web page is http://www.protech-inc.com.

Entering the URL address on the screen transfers the user to a Web page. Some Web sites have multiple pages where the first page is called the "home page." Many Web pages offer additional sources of information called hyperlinks that are highlighted in various colors. A mouse click on the words or graphic sends the user directly to the new Web page. Some suppliers offer online catalogs of their products. Pricing may also appear on the Web page, but should be confirmed before ordering.

A buyer could spend many hours trying to guess what a potential supplier's Internet address is. Fortunately there are search tools, called search engines, that can help the buyer find an organization. These engines which have URL addresses of their own (see Appendix viii) will scan databases of Internet addresses for a name or product or term that the buyer wants. Understanding the search logic each one uses and finding a particular product or service may take the buyer a while at first. The best approach is to start as broadly as possible and then narrow the search.

Suppose a buyer wanted to find stainless steel sheet suppliers. Using a search engine, type in "metal," "stainless," and "steel." This will lead the buyer to another Web page that has a listing of stainless suppliers. It is not unusual to have to bounce through several different Web sites to find the information required. Most Internet software allows the user to save a particular Web site so he or she can quickly call it up without having to go through several pages. There are also online networks and catalogs the buyer can use.

Thomas Registers is online and, at present, offers free access to their database (http://www. thomasregister.com). Also, a service called Industry Net (http://www.industry.net) offers free access to network of suppliers and supplier catalogs that can be searched by product or name. Both of these Web sites found stainless steel sheet suppliers faster than the search engines. However, only companies that have paid a subscription are on the services. Search engines will usually find almost all vendors who have a web page, but will take longer. There is software, called intelligent agent browsers, being developed that will make searching easier.

While many public and private organizations are rushing to develop Web sites to market their products and services, it should be noted that not all suppliers have Web pages. The high-tech companies and suppliers will be more likely to have a Web page than the lower tech organizations.

Where Is Purchasing Today?

Most Purchasing departments are just starting to use the Internet. A recent survey by CommerceNet and N.A.P.M. — Silicon Valley[2] noted that 55% of the survey participants classified themselves as "beginners." Over 75% estimated that less than 25% of their suppliers were online. Most respondents used the Internet to browse through catalogs, post RFQs or RFIs and for e-mail (to check order status and for some limited purchase order transmission). The small number of respondents (20) demonstrates even more than the data that most buyers are not aware of this potentially significant resource for finding sources of supply.

Cautions And Risks Of Using The Internet

The Internet, like any tool, can be misused. Identifying potential suppliers and making bid packages available to all suppliers is one of the great advantages of the Internet. The Internet can also provide the buyer with certain financial data through supplier home pages and other services such as Dun and Bradstreet. However, qualifying suppliers still requires the buyer to have hands-on involvement. A supplier can make any claim on its Web page. In addition, electronic vandals can also tamper with Web pages since most Web server systems are not secure. It is up to the buyer or buying team to decide if the supplier is viable and is the best cost producer.

Commerce on the Internet (called e-commerce) is still in its infancy. It currently lacks standardized security and transaction and payment systems. This has begun to change. According to David Angell,[3] several secure-transaction systems are or will be available on the Internet to support commerce.

One of these systems is called a session-level security protocol. Several versions are currently available and a based upon the public key encryption system (see Appendix viii). They provide a method for encrypting communications between servers (computers where the Web pages are located) and Web browsers. These protocols provide the framework for encryption, authentication and digital signatures (i.e., is the party on the other end legitimate and are they who they say they are?). These protocols can protect purchasing or credit card numbers sent across the Web, but they don't provide the necessary means for securely handling the financial transactions (payment, etc.) between the consumer and the financial institution. Another system is needed to accomplish this.

Visa and Mastercard have recently agreed-upon a standard for keeping online transactions secure from user to financial institution. Called Secure Electronic Transaction (SET), it is based on the widely used Data Encryption Standard (DES) and supports the public-key encryption and other standards. It is designed only to protect financial information, not e-mail or other types of computer documents such as drawings. It should be noted that this system will not be available until December 1996 at the earliest.

Conclusion

The Internet can be a useful tool to identify potential suppliers. Qualifying suppliers is still up to the buyer and his or her buying team. Tools to conduct secure e-commerce are not yet available. Angell states ". . . the operative words of Net-Based commerce are wait, look and listen."[4] However, the buyer can use the Internet now to locate sources of supply on a worldwide scale.

Costs are minimal compared to the potential benefits. Purchasing departments need to present a strong case to top management to get immediate access to the Internet to remain competitive by finding the best cost suppliers in today's global marketplace.

[1]   "Laying the Track," David Angell, *Internet World*, August 1996, p. 36.
[2]   "Internet Impact on Procurement," CommerceNet and N.A.P.M. — Silicon Valley, May 1996, http://www.catalog.com/napmsv/ipurch3.htm.
[3]   "Laying the Track," David Angell, *Internet World*, August 1996, pp. 34, 36.
[4]   "Laying the Track," David Angell, *Internet World*, August 1996, p. 36.

THE
BIDDING
PROCESS

CHAPTER SIX

The sourcing process does not stop with locating potential sources of supply. The next question a buyer should ask is: "Are they viable sources of supply?" In other words, can they make/supply the product/service needed? If the buyer is familiar with potential suppliers or has used them before to fill similar needs, then the answer may be a quick "yes." This would also be true, if the suppliers are on an "Approved Supplier List" for the product/service needed. These suppliers are considered "preapproved" before the bid is sent out. On the other hand, if one or more potential suppliers is new or has no experience providing the buyer with the product or service needed, the bidding process can help "weed out" the unqualified or nonviable sources. The bidding process also provides the product/service description and quantity requirements as well as technical, quality and other information.

Overview Of The Bidding Process

1) The bidding process documents the defined needs informa-

tion covered in Chapter One (What is needed? When is it needed? Who needs it?), putting the information in one package. Standard, and any special, terms and condition are also included. Making sure the package accurately describes what is needed is the joint responsibility of the buyer and the requester. This package can be as short as one page or many hundreds of pages depending upon the requirements and complexity of the product or service being bid.

2) The package is sent to the identified potential sources of supply (whether preapproved or not) with a time limit for them to respond. This solicitation is variously called an Invitation For Bid (IFB), a Request For Quote (RFQ), or a Request For Proposal (RFP) depending upon whether the requester is a government or private entity. The term "RFP" is more often used if the specifications are unknown or uncertain.

3) Written records should be kept concerning who is bidding, when the package was sent, etc.

4) All potential suppliers must be treated equally. Any questions or clarification requests (including requested changes to the bid) from the potential suppliers should be written down and the responses, if they affect the bid in any way, should be shared with the other suppliers.

5) Normally the bidding documentation should be kept for at least three to seven years in case any questions arise concerning the process.

Some organizations, particularly those in the government/public sector, require a rigorous bidding process with complete written documentation of all the steps and actions associated with the bid. Other organizations have less strict requirements. It should be noted that many purchasing departments have polices and procedures in place to instruct a buyer on how to handle the bidding process. When in doubt, a buyer should consult his or her purchasing manager or the organization's legal department or legal representative before the bidding process is started.

Competitive, Noncompetitive, And Two-Step Bidding

There are three types of bidding — competitive (multiple supplier possibilities), noncompetitive (sole source/negotiation) and two-step bidding. All follow the basic bid procedure outlined above, but should be used under different supplier marketplace circumstances and buyer requirements.

Competitive Bidding

It is obvious that competitive bidding (multiple suppliers) can only be used when the supplier marketplace has an "adequate" number of suppliers. Depending upon the competitiveness of the supplier base, the definition of "adequate" may mean two suppliers or it may mean more than two. There are additional considerations as well. The specifications (whether performance-based or otherwise) for what the buyer wants should be clear to both the buyer and potential suppliers. The potential suppliers must have the know-how and capabilities to provide the product or service, as well as the interest (it must be worth the suppliers' time and expense to prepare a reply), in vying for the buyer's business. Suppliers must also have the time to evaluate the bid and respond. Rushing a bid can result in inaccurate costs, delivery dates, etc. The buyer will also need time to evaluate the replies.

Some buyers do not recommend competitive bidding if the costs are uncertain due to: high-tech requirements or extremely long lead-times, situations where price is not the most important or one of the most important factors, uncertainty in design specifications, or special setup or tooling costs are a major cost factor. Costing unknowns and uncertainty in the design specifications can create "apples to oranges" problems when is comes to evaluating the bid. However, using the weighted evaluation methods discussed in the next chapter, the buyer can address the price importance factor concern. Life cycle costing or piece part amortization methods can eliminate the challenges associated with setup or tooling costs.

Disadvantages of Competitive Bidding

There are some disadvantages or drawbacks when using the competitive bidding approach. Perhaps the two biggest are that cost can become the overriding factor and that the amount of time required for the process.

When used properly, the competitive bidding system normally identifies the most cost-efficient supplier. Problems arise when the cost factor of the product overrides all other factors such as quality, delivery, supplier partnerships, etc. Suppliers are not going to enter into long-term relationships if the buyer or organization has a reputation for "cost first, last, and always." A short-term cost savings can jeopardize larger, longer-term savings in maintenance costs, reliability, quality, etc. Used incorrectly, competitive bidding can destroy supplier partnerships which rely on a long-term relationship that is beneficial to both parties and where cost is only one factor in the relationship.

As mentioned above, time is required for the supplier to review and put together a bid and the buyer to evaluate the bid. The more complex the RFQ, the more time it will take for the suppliers to reply and the buyer to evaluate it. Based on this parameter, rush orders generally should not be competitively bid.

It should be noted that this is true for governmental organizations as well as private firms. For example, under a declared state of emergency (weather or other reason), governmental requirements for competitively bidding goods and services can be suspended.

Ethics of Competitive Bidding

As mentioned previously, all potential suppliers should be treated equally. Any questions from suppliers or other changes that alter the bid must be given to all suppliers at the same time. Time extensions should be granted to all suppliers or to no suppliers. The buyer must always be impartial, fair and above board in both appearance and reality.

There are other ethical considerations as well. For example, all bidders who did not get the business should be notified in a timely fashion. How they are notified varies widely. Many governmental bids are awarded publicly at the bid opening. Trade journals and other news media are sometimes notified. In addition to these methods, some government awards (particularly federal) are published by several for-profit subscription services. Private business tends to be less formal, ranging from a formal letter to a verbal telephone call. Some buyers use a style of "If you haven't heard from me by such and such a date, you didn't get it." Some suppliers find this approach demeaning and insulting and may be less willing to respond to future requests for quote. If the buyer opts for the informal method, a better approach might be, "Feel free to call me after such and such a date, and I'll let you know."

There is a difference of opinion among purchasing professionals concerning whether it is ethical to give bidders pricing and other feedback after the bid is closed or awarded. In the case of most public purchasing, information about the bid is required to be made available to all bidders, as well as the public at large. Private firms are usually not required to be as open. Some buyers will release the information if they want to promote more price competition. Others feel that the information should be considered confidential and will only tell the name of the winning suppliers. In the case of a supplier's proprietary process, where revealing pricing information can be detrimental to the supplier, the latter approach should be used. Letting the suppliers know up front if their bids will be made public is the professional and ethical thing to do.

Ethics is never a cut and dried issue. The individual buyer may have to make judgment calls. Fortunately for the buyer, the more advanced purchasing departments have polices and procedures available to guide the buyer. Contacting other purchasing professionals is another way to get advice. Generally speaking, the Golden Rule of "doing unto others as you would have others do unto you" is a good preliminary yardstick.

Noncompetitive Bidding

In some cases, particularly with purchase requests that have unclear specifications, delivery dates, and/or cost parameters or when a sole source situation exists, competitive bidding is not possible or will not generate a "best buy" situation. Under these circumstances it is better to negotiate with the supplier and avoid cost overruns, missed delivery dates or paying too much. Sellers unsure of the labor and materials needed to fill a requirement may tend to "pad" the bid to allow for unknown direct and indirect costs. Also, if the buyer's organization has entered into Supplier Partnerships, Strategic Sourcing Agreements or Early Supplier Involvement programs that create a sole source situation, negotiation may be the only approach for the buyer.

A bid (formal or informal) should still be generated since it clarifies (as much as possible) what the buyer wants. The supplier will respond to the request with an offer or counteroffer. It is up to the buyer to use good negotiating techniques (including cost/price analysis, market analysis, etc.) to reach a best buy agreement with the seller.

Disadvantages of Noncompetitive Bidding

Generally speaking, the buyer must have good negotiating skills and be more vigilant to avoid being taken advantage of in a noncompetitive bidding situation. The disadvantages of noncompetitive bidding are covered in greater detail in Chapter 2 under sole and multiple sourcing.

Two-Step Bidding

When specifications are insufficient or not clear or the requirement pushes existing technology, a buyer might want to employ the two-step bidding process. Government entities tend to use this process more than private firms. The buyer should notify all potential suppliers that he or she is going to use the two-step process in the initial bid. In the first step, a bid is prepared which requests technical proposals (usually without pricing information). The second step is the normal competitive bidding situation (pricing, delivery, quality, etc.), but it is offered only to the suppliers who presented suitable technical responses in the first step. The final award is usually based on price since all the second-round bidders have passed the technical phase.

In some cases, the lowest bidder gets the business if all other terms and conditions (quality, delivery, etc.) are met. In other cases, the second step is the start of a negotiation process. This is particularly true if all suppliers cannot meet the terms and conditions of the second bid. Ethics requires that the potential suppliers be notified at the beginning which method the buyer intends to use.

Disadvantages of Two-Step Bidding

Two-step bidding takes more time than the other two methods. If time is an important consideration, then the buyer should use one of the other processes. Also, the extra evaluation step requires more purchasing time and associated costs. Sometimes the two-step process becomes a three or more step process with buyers and suppliers wasting time and money. Due to the added time and cost factors, the experienced buyer will only use the two-step process if competitive bidding or noncompetitive bidding will not yield a best buy scenario.

Conclusion

Making sure that specifications and other terms and conditions accurately describe requirements is the job of both the buyer and requester. Both parties bring particular expertise to the process. A bid package that accurately describes what is needed at the beginning of the bid process makes the evaluation and selection of the supplier easier and less time consuming. Having to go back and clarify a supplier's bid due to ambiguities in the bid package is time consuming and increases processing costs. Selecting the proper bid process, based on marketplace conditions and what is being purchased, is crucial since the buyer can use the correct strategy to achieve a best buy situation. Evaluating and selecting bids is covered in the next chapter.

EVALUATING
AND
SELECTING SOURCES

CHAPTER SEVEN

The next step in sourcing is to evaluate the suppliers and their bid(s) and select a source. Generally speaking, suppliers are evaluated on price, quality, delivery and service, though additional factors, such as social responsibility, may be added. In some cases, evaluation and selection can be simple — in a competitive bid, one supplier appears to be clearly superior; in a two-step bid, the field has narrowed to one supplier, etc. In cases where the evaluation is not cut and dried, the buyer will need some tools in his or her purchasing toolkit to help identify the best buy. For simplicity, this chapter will break out the evaluation and selection into two types – noncompetitive or sole source supplier and multiple suppliers.

Noncompetitive/Sole Source

At first glance, an uninitiated buyer might conclude that there is nothing to evaluate on a sole source bid. The experienced buyer will use the bid as a basis of negotiation. While negotiation techniques are beyond the scope of this book (see *The World of Negotiations: Never Being a Loser*, PT Publications, for detailed information),

---

the bid evaluation techniques below can be used to establish beginning negotiating positions. Price analysis or cost analysis can be used to evaluate the price component. Quality can be analyzed by reviewing the supplier's past performance and is sometimes quantified as a cost adder (one simple method takes the reject percentage and adds it to the total price by multiplying the bid price times 1 + %). Delivery and service evaluations also rely on past performance. It should be noted that if the sole source situation has been created by a supplier partnership, then quality, delivery and service performance must already meet or exceed the requirements and are not factors in the evaluation. If pricing was not included in the partnership agreement, then pricing is the only issue.

Price Analysis

Aside from commodities where prices are set by statute or regulation (such as electric power rates), traditional price analysis for sole sourcing relies on either historical pricing, catalog/price listings or by the buyer's own analysis. Each method has some potential drawbacks that may not insure a best buy.

Historical pricing relies on comparison of the bid price with prices paid in the past for an equal or approximately equal good or service. "Approximately equal" can create an "apples to oranges" comparison that may not be valid. With invalid comparisons, the buyer could leave some money on the table; negotiate the seller down to an unrealistic price with possible negative impacts on quality or other factors; or have the seller decide not to do business with the buyer at all.

Even assuming equality, historical pricing can still lead a buyer astray. How much inflation or deflation has taken place since the last order and what index should a buyer use to quantify the amount? Basing it on a standard inflation gauge such as the Producer Price Index may not be valid for a particular commodity or industry. Take for example electronic microprocessors. They have historically dropped in price over an average life-span of three to five years even though the Producer Price Index has increased. Furthermore, they can be subjected to wild swings in demand creating temporary gluts or shortages that can dramatically affect the pricing structure.

Catalog or price listings can be misleading as well. First, the buyer needs to have the supplier document that recent sales of the commodity and the quantity of the commodity have been sold at a given price to many other customers. It can be illegal to do otherwise, but this will not protect the buyer from unscrupulous sellers. Secondly, catalogs and price listings are usually dated, but can be superseded at anytime by the seller (sometimes without notice). Finally, depending upon the product being purchased, the buyer may be paying too much if he or she pays the listed price. For example, no savvy buyer will pay the manufacturer's suggested retail price for a car.

The buyer can do his or her own price analysis, sometimes using his or her own expertise of the product and the product's marketplace, or just using an educated guess. The drawback to using a buyer's own price analysis is that it may not be practical or accurate. However in some cases it is an acceptable method. For example, a buyer was tasked with finding a replacement car for a manager. It had to be a certain make and model and be considered "new" for financial purposes. She discovered a one-year-old car with only 200 miles on it qualifying it as a "new" car. Blue Book value of the car (a standard method of pricing used cars) wasn't applicable due to the low mileage. On the other hand it wasn't a current model car, so the listed price wasn't accurate either. The salesman insisted on telling her about a leasing plan where the dealer would offer to sell her company the car after two years for approximately 50% of the list price. Using the dealer's logic, the buyer calculated that a one year old car would be worth 75% of the list price and set her negotiation price ceiling accordingly.

If, for whatever reason, a buyer cannot reach a reasonable price using the analysis methods above, he or she should use Cost Analysis.

Cost Analysis

Cost Analysis looks at the actual or anticipated costs associated with providing a good or service. Some buyers require suppliers to provide cost data as part of their supplier partnership agreements. The object of the exercise is to arrive at a price that is fair for both buyer and seller. All costs (direct, indirect, tooling or setup, learning curves, etc.) and profit are quantified. Obviously this requires the trust and cooperation of the supplier and buyer. Both parties must be willing to provide each other with private and other sensitive data about their respective operations if Cost Analysis is to succeed.

Direct costs include all the direct labor and direct material costs used to create the finished product. Any scrap or rework cost is also added. Indirect costs include selling, general and administrative, engineering (if any), manufacturing and materials handling overheads. The final component is profit. Buyers and sellers can

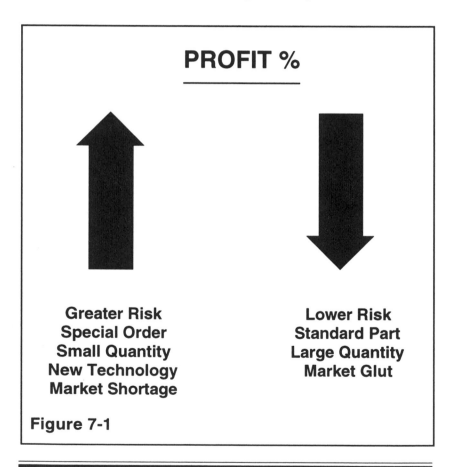

PROFIT %

Greater Risk   **Lower Risk**
Special Order   **Standard Part**
Small Quantity   **Large Quantity**
New Technology   **Market Glut**
Market Shortage

Figure 7-1

usually quantify and reach a quick agreement on direct and indirect costs, but what constitutes a "fair" profit can be a contentious issue. The seller wants to maximize his profits while the buyer wants to keep price low. Profit margins will vary depending upon the what is being bought and the current market conditions. The chart on the preceding page (Figure 7-1) offers the buyer some guidelines when calculating profit.

Price and Cost Analysis tools can be used for competitive and two-step bidding as well, but the competition created by the multiple supplier bid method tends to make the suppliers more price competitive.

Multiple Suppliers

Evaluating and selecting a supplier from multiple bids usually requires more time and work than for a sole source bid. Not only are there more bids to review, but the issues of quality, delivery and service may vary as well as price. Many buyers like to create spreadsheets to evaluate multiple bids using a weighted factor system. Factors (price, delivery, quality, service, etc.) are identified and rated according to importance. The ratings usually

BID EVALUATION WEIGHTED FACTOR METHOD

Factor	Max. Rating	Supplier 1	Supplier 2	Supplier 3
Price	30	25	28	27
Quality	30	22	21	25
Delivery	30	29	25	26
Service	10	5	6	7
Total Rating	100	81	80	85

Figure 7-2

add up to 100 or 100%. Figure 7-2 is an example of this method. Notice that Supplier 2 had the best price (i.e., highest rating), but would not get the job since the overall highest rating was Supplier 3.

The weighted factors used may vary depending upon circumstances (what is being bought, when is it needed, etc.). Deciding which factors to use and how important they are to the total bid should be decided before the bid is sent out. There doesn't appear to be any consensus among buyers as to who in the organization decides the factors and assigns the weight. Those firms with Total Quality Management (TQM) or team environments tend to let a team decide. In other organizations, the buyer or purchasing manager sets the criteria. As a general rule, the team approach should be used for more complex bids to make sure that the proper expertise is utilized to help assure a best buy situation.

Information about the bid analysis, the factors and their respective weights should be included in the bid package. This will help the suppliers provide an accurate response and will avoid the appearance of favoritism.

BID EVALUATION UNIT COST FACTOR METHOD

Factor	X Price	Supplier 1	Supplier 2	Supplier 3
Bid Price		100	95	93
Quality	1 - % reject	14 86%	15 85%	12 88%
Delivery	1 - % on time	3 97%	7 93%	5 95%
Service	1 - % problem orders	50 50%	40 60%	30 70%
Total Cost		168.83	158.78	141.83

Figure 7-3

Some buyers prefer to use a method that quantifies unit costs associated with each factor. Mary Lu Harding uses unit cost to quantify quality and on-time delivery[1] as well as lead-time and the social and environmental issues[2] discussed in Chapter Three. Using Harding's method, Figure 7-2 would look something like Figure 7-3.

Some buyers prefer to customize a bid evaluation based upon specific requirements of the product or service being bought. Appendix vii shows an example for evaluating computer software and hardware. A buyer probably wouldn't want to custom evaluate every bid since it takes time and effort to create an evaluation form. Also, if the criteria for evaluation keep changing, suppliers might get confused and frustrated and decide that the buyer's business is not worth the effort. However, for one-of-a-kind or large dollar nonrepeating purchases, a customized evaluation can be very helpful.

Conclusion

Whatever system the buyer or buying team decides upon should be consistently applied. Potential suppliers should be notified in advance concerning how the bid will be evaluated. Whether or not the buyer shares the evaluations with the bidders has been covered in Chapter Five under ethics of competitive bidding. Using consistent evaluation systems can help the buyer provide the best buy scenario that is expected by his or her organization whether it is a sole sourced or multiple sourced product or service.

---

[1] "Calculating Unit Total Cost," Mary Lu Harding, *Purchasing Today*, May 1996, p. 12.

[2] "Piece of the Puzzle," Mary Lu Harding, *Purchasing Today*, July 1996, pp. 14-15.

ALWAYS LOOKING

CHAPTER EIGHT

Always looking for new or better sourcing is part of every buyer's job of finding the best cost suppliers for his or her organization. Sometimes it can be a time consuming exercise. And all buyers are faced with a plethora of terms which are not completely understood. *The Glossary of Key Purchasing Terms, Acronyms, and Formulas* (PT Publications) defines them, so that you will be armed with all the necessary information. Some buyers, feeling pressured just to handle the day-to-day requisitions and the other "normal" work load requirements, feel they don't have time to be constantly looking for new sources. Other buyers who have long-term supplier agreements are sometimes lulled into thinking that they don't have to look for new suppliers either. Both groups are taking a short-term approach to the job of purchasing that can have adverse effects on their organizations and their careers.

Buyers who think they don't have the time to spend or the need to be looking for the best cost supplier might want to ask themselves, "If I don't keep looking:

1) **How will I know I am getting the best buy (price, delivery, quality and service)?**
2) **How can I prove to top management that we are buying competitively?**
3) **How will I know if there are better ways or methods of obtaining goods and services for my organization?**
4) **How can I be sure I am doing all I can to help my organization reach its goals?**
5) **How do I find out about new techniques, technologies and products?"**

One final question, "If I don't keep looking for new sources, how can I justify keeping my job in tight times?"

Gerald Egan states "... it is not enough to do what is required. You must keep finding ways to add value to the business. To stay with us, you must be a contributor rather than a mere player. . . To remain a contributor you must grow and develop."[1]

By constantly looking for new and better suppliers, the buyer can add value to his or her organization and enhance his or her career.

---

[1]   "Hard Times: What's In Store for Employee Contracts?" Gerald Egan, *Management Today*, Jan. 1994, pp. 48-51.

SMALL **B**USINESS **A**DMINISTRATION **B**USINESS **I**NFORMATION **C**ENTERS (BICs)[1] AS OF **1/97**

APPENDIX I

ALABAMA
No Announced Plans

ALASKA
No Announced Plans

ARIZONA
Phoenix – 1997

ARKANSAS
Little Rock – 1997

CALIFORNIA
Business Information Centers
(BICs)

U.S. Small Business
Administration

Business Information Center
Attn: Ken Davis
3600 Wilshire Blvd., Suite L100
Los Angeles, CA 90010
(213) 251-7253 voice
(213) 251-7255 fax

U.S. Small Business
Administration
San Diego District Office
Attn: Teddy Luszcz
550 West C Street, Suite 550
San Diego, CA 92101
(619) 557-7252 voice
(619) 557-5894 fax

Business Information Center
Southwestern College
Attn. Ken Clark
900 Otay Lake Road
Chula Vista, CA 91910
(619) 482-6375 voice
(619) 482-6402 fax

The Entrepreneur Center
U.S. Small Business
Administration
Attn. Katherine Butler-Tom
211 Main Street, 4th Floor
San Francisco, CA 94105-1988
(415) 744-4242 voice
(415) 744-9812 fax

COLORADO
Business Information Center
(BIC)

U.S. Small Business
Administration
Denver District Office
Attn: Cyndi Jones
721 19th Street, Suite 426
Denver, CO 80202-2599
(303) 844-3986 voice
(303) 844-6468 fax

CONNECTICUT
Business Information Center
(BIC)

Connecticut Small Business –
Key to the Future, Inc.
Business Information Center
Hartford Civic Center
Attn: James Williams

1 Civic Center Plaza, Suite 301
Hartford, CT 06103
(860) 251-7000 voice
(860) 251-7006 fax

DELAWARE
Business Information Center
(BIC)

Delaware Small Business
Resource and Information
Center
Attn: Kai Brunswick
1318 N. Market Street
Wilmington, DE 19801
(302) 831-1555 voice
(302) 831-1423 fax

DISTRICT OF COLUMBIA
Business Information Center
(BIC)

SBA/Bell Atlantic
Business Information Center
Washington District Office
Attn: Joyce Howard
1110 Vermont Avenue N.W.,
Suite 900
Washington, DC 20043-4500
(202) 606-4000 ext. 266 voice
(202) 606-4225 fax

FLORIDA
Miami - Projected Opening
Spring 1997

GEORGIA
Business Information Center
(BIC)

U.S. Small Business Administration
Atlanta District Office
Attn: Fred Brandt
1720 Peachtree Rd., NW, 6th Fl.
Atlanta, GA 30309
(404) 347-4749 voice
(404) 347-2355 fax

GUAM
No Announced Plans

HAWAII
Business Information Center
(BIC)

Business Information Center
(BIC)
Bancorp
Attn: Jane Sawyer
130 Merchant Street, Suite 1030
Honolulu, HA 96850-4981
(808) 522-8131 voice
(808) 541-3650 fax

IDAHO
Business Information Center
(BIC)

U.S. Small Business Administration
Boise District Office
Attn: Sherrie Sugden
1020 Main Street
Boise, ID 83702-5745
(208) 334-9077 voice
(208) 334-9353 fax

ILLINOIS
Business Information Center
(BIC)

U.S. Small Business Administration
Chicago District Office
Attn: Phyllis Scott
500 W. Madison Street, Suite 1250
Chicago, IL 60661-2511
(312) 353-1825 voice
(312) 886-5688 fax

INDIANA
Indianapolis – in 1997

IOWA
No Announced Plans

KANSAS
Wichita – in 1997

KENTUCKY
Business Information Center
(BIC)

The One Stop Capital Shop
(OSCS)
The Center for Rural Development
2292 S. Hwy. 27, Suite 275
Somerset, Kentucky 42501
(606) 677-6080 voice
(606) 677-6081 fax

LOUISIANA
Planned in 1997

MAINE
Business Information Center
(BIC)

Business Information Center of
Maine
The Bates Mill Complex
Attn: Bonnie Erickson
35 Canal Street
Lewiston, ME 04240
(207) 782-5335 voice
(207) 783 7745 fax

MARYLAND
Business Information Center
(BIC)

SBA/NationsBank/MBDA/Bell
Atlantic
Small Business Resource Center
Attn: Rachel Howard
3 West Baltimore Street
Corner of Charles & Baltimore
Baltimore, MD 21201
(410) 605-0990 voice
(410) 605-0995 fax

MASSACHUSETTS
Business Information Center
(BIC)

U.S. Small Business
Administration
Boston District Office
Attn: Andrea Ross
10 Causeway Street, Room 265
Boston, MA 02222-1093
(617) 565-5615 voice
(617) 565-5598 fax

MICHIGAN
No Announced Plans

MINNESOTA
Minneapolis - Projected
Opening 1997

MISSISSIPPI
No Announced Plans

MISSOURI
Business Information Centers
(BICs)

U.S. Small Business Information
Center
Kansas City District Office
Attn: Kim Malcolm
323 West 8th Street, Suite 104
Kansas City, MO 64105
(816) 374-6675 voice
(816) 374-6759 fax

Business Information Center
Attn: Seymour Shuler
121 S. Meramec Avenue
Lobby Level
St. Louis, MO 63105
(314) 854-6861 voice
(314) 889-7687 fax

U.S. Small Business
Administration
Kansas City District Office
Attn: Kim Malcolm
323 West 8th Street, Suite 104
Kansas City, MO 64105
(816) 374-6675 voice
(816) 374-6759 fax

MONTANA
Business Information Center
(BIC)

U.S. Small Business Administration
Business Information Center
Attn: Robert Much
301 South Park, Room 334
Helena, MO 63105
(406) 441 1081 voice
(406) 441-1090 fax

NEBRASKA
Business Information Center
(BIC)

U.S. Small Business
Administration
Business Information Center
Attn: Jan Allen
11141 Mill Valley Road
Omaha, NE 68154
(402) 221-3606 voice
(402) 221-3680 fax

NEVADA
Las Vegas – 1997

NEW HAMPSHIRE
No Announced Plans

NEW JERSEY
Business Information Center
(BIC)

Business Information Center
U.S. Small Business

Administration
Attn: Frank Burke
2 Gateway Center, 4th Floor
Newark, NJ 07102
(201) 645-6049 voice
(201) 645-6265 fax

NEW MEXICO
Albuquerque - Projected
Opening Spring 1997

NEW YORK
Business Information Center
(BIC)

The Capital Resource Center
Attn: Daniel O'Connell
1 Computer Drive
Albany, NY 12205
(518) 446-1118 Ext. 31 voice
(518) 446-1228 fax

NORTH CAROLINA
SBA/NationsBank/MBDA/
U.S. Small Business
Administration
Attn: Eileen Joyce
200 North College Street
Suite A 2015
Charlotte, NC 28202-2137
(704) 344-9797 voice
(704) 344-6769 fax

NORTH DAKOTA
Native American Reservations –
 In Planning Stages

OHIO
Cleveland – 1997

OKLAHOMA
Business Information Center
(BIC)

U.S. Small Business Administration
Business Information Center
Attn: Maria Barnaba-Moore
UCO Small Business Development Center
115 Park Avenue
Oklahoma City, OK 73102
(405) 232-1968 voice

OREGON
Business Information Centers
(BICs)

Confederated Tribes
of the Warm Springs
Economic Development Office
Attn: David Dona
1103 Wasco Street
Warm Springs, OR 97761
(503) 553-3592 voice
(541) 553-3593 fax

Confederated Tribes
of the Grand Ronde Community
9615 Grand Ronde Rd.
Grand Ronde, OR 97347
Attn: Doug Hampton
(503) 879-5211 voice
(503) 879-2479 fax

The Klamath Tribes
414 Chocktoot Street
Chiloquin, OR 97624
Attn: Gordon Thompson
(503) 783-2219 voice
(541) 783-2029 fax

PENNSYLVANIA
No Announced Plans

PUERTO RICO
No Announced Plans

RHODE ISLAND
Business Information Centers
(BICs)

U.S. Small Business
Administration
Business Information Center
Attn: Patricia O'Rouke
380 West Minister Mall, Rm. 511
Providence, RI 02903
(401) 528-4688 voice
(401) 528-4539 fax

Enterprise Community College
Attn: Yvette McCray
3550 Broad Street
Providence, RI 02907
(401) 272-1083 voice
(401) 272-1186 fax

SOUTH CAROLINA
Business Information Center
(BIC)

SBA/NationsBank/MBDA/
BellSouth/College of Charleston
Small Business Resource Center
Attn: Kit Rogers
284 King Street
Charleston, SC 29401
(803) 853-3900 voice
(803) 853-2529 fax

SOUTH DAKOTA
Native American Reservations -
In Planning Stages

TENNESSEE
Business Information Center
(BIC)

SBA/NationsBank/MBDA
Small Business Resource Center
Attn: Lilly Taylor
3401 West End Avenue
Nashville, TN 37203
(615) 749-4000 voice
(615) 749-3685 fax

TEXAS
Business Information Centers
(BICs)

U.S. Small Business
Administration
Houston District Office
Attn: Neil Blanton
9301 Southwest Freeway, Ste. 550
Houston, TX 77074-1591
(713) 773-6518 voice
(713) 773-6550 fax

U.S. General Store for Small
Business
Attn: Neal Blanton
5400 Grigts
Houston, Texas 77021
(713) 643-8000 voice
(713) 643-8193 fax

U.S. Small Business Administra-
tion/Fort Worth Business Assistance Center
Attn: David Edmonds

100 East 15th Street, Suite 400
Fort Worth, TX 76102
(817) 871-6007 voice
(817) 871-6031 fax

SBA/Greater El Paso
Chamber of Commerce
Business Information Center
Mindy Vinnarreal
Ten Civic Center Plaza
El Paso, TX 79901
(915) 534-0531 voice
(915) 534-0513 fax

UTAH
Business Information Center
(BIC)

Utah Technology Finance
Corporation
Attn: Suzan Yoshimura
117 East 100 South
Salt Lake City, UT 84111
(801) 364-1331 voice

VERMONT
Business Information Center
(BIC)

Business Information Center
Vermont Technical College
Hartness Library
Attn: Bernie Villemaier
Randolph Center, Vermont
05061
(802) 728-1231 voice
(802) 728-1237 fax

VIRGINIA
Richmond - Projected Opening
Early 1997

WASHINGTON
Business Information Centers
(BICs)

U.S. Small Business Administration
Seattle District Office
Attn: Doreen White
1200 Sixth Avenue, Suite 1700
Seattle, WA 98101-1128
(206) 553-7310 voice
(206) 553-7099 fax

SBA / Spokane Chamber of Commerce
Business Information Center
Attn: Coralie Myers
1020 W. Riverside
Spokane, WA 99201
(509) 353-2630 voice
(509) 353-2600 fax

WEST VIRGINIA
Business Information Center
(BIC)

SBA/WVHTC Foundation
Business Information Center
Attn: Nick Lambernedis
200 Fairmont Avenue, 3rd Floor
Fairmont, WV 26554
(304) 366-2577 ext. 111 voice
(304) 366-2699 fax

WISCONSIN
No Announced Plans

WYOMING
Casper - 1997

1   Small Business Administration:
http://www.sbaonline.sba.gov/gopher/Local-Information/Business-Information-Centers/

OFFICES
OF SMALL AND
DISADVANTAGED
BUSINESS
UTILIZATION

APPENDIX II

Note: Offices designated as Offices of Small and Disadvantaged Business Utilization (OSDBUs) provide procurement assistance to small, minority, 8(a) and women-owned businesses. Their primary function is to ensure that small and disadvantaged businesses receive their fair share of U.S. Government contracts. "OSDBUs" are the contacts for their respective agencies and are excellent sources of information.

AGENCY FOR INTERNA-
TIONAL DEVELOPMENT
Room 1200A SA-14
Washington, DC 20523-1414
(703) 875-1551 voice
(703) 875-1862 fax
Attn: Mr. Ivan R. Ashley,
Director, OSDBU

BUREAU OF INDIAN AFFAIRS
Division of Contracting and
Grants Administration
1849 C Street, N.W.,
Mail Stop 334-SIB
Washington, DC 20240
(202) 208-2825 voice
(202) 219-4071 fax
Attn: Ms. Stephenita Devlin,
Procurement Analyst

CORPORATION FOR
NATIONAL SERVICE
1225 New York Avenue, N.W.,
Rm. 6107
Washington, DC 20525
(202) 606-5000, ext. 404 or 403
voice
(202) 565-2777 or 2778 fax
Attn: Mr. Norman Franklin,
Director Office of Procurement
and Administrative Services

DEFENSE LOGISTICS AGENCY
HEADQUARTERS
DDAS/Office of Small and Disadvantaged Business Utilization
8725 John J. Kingman Road, Suite
2533
Ft. Belvoir, VA 22060-6221
(703) 767-1650 voice
(703) 767-1670 fax
Attn: Mr. Lloyd C. Alderman,
Director, OSDBU

DEPARTMENT OF
AGRICULTURE
14th and Independence Ave.,
S.W., Room 1323, South Bldg.
Washington, DC 20250
(202) 720-7117 voice
(202) 720-3001 fax
Attn: Ms. Sharron Harris, Director,
OSDBU

DEPARTMENT OF COMMERCE
14th and Constitution Ave., N.W.
Room H-6411
Washington, DC 20230
(202) 482-1472 voice
(202) 482-0501 fax
Attn: Mr. Michael Keane, Acting
Director, OSDBU

DEPARTMENT OF DEFENSE
Office of Small and Disadvantaged
Business Utilization
3061 Defense Pentagon, Room
2A338
Washington, DC 20301-3061
(703) 697-1688 voice
(703) 693-7014 fax
Attn: Ms. Susan E. Haley, Acting
Director, OSDBU

DEPARTMENT OF
EDUCATION
7th and D Street, S.W., Rm. 3120,
ROB-3
Washington, DC 20202-0521
(202) 708-9820 voice
(202) 401-6477 fax
Attn: Ms. Marcella Coverson,
Acting Director, OSDBU

DEPARTMENT OF ENERGY
1000 Independence Avenue, S.W.,
Room 4B080
Washington, DC 20585
(202) 586-7377 voice
(202) 586-5488 fax
Attn: Mr. Percy McCraney,
Deputy Director, OSDBU (ED-3)

DEPARTMENT OF HEALTH AND HUMAN SERVICES
200 Independence Ave., S.W., Room 517D, Humphrey Building
Washington, DC 20201
(202) 690-7300 voice
(202) 690-8772 fax
Attn: Mr. Verl Zanders, Director, OSDBU

DEPARTMENT OF HOUSING AND URBAN DEVELOPMENT
451 7th Street, S.W., Room 3130
Washington, DC 20410
(202) 708-1428 voice
(202) 708-7642 fax
Attn: Mr. Joseph Piljay, Small Business Specialist

DEPARTMENT OF JUSTICE
1331 Pennsylvania Avenue, N.W.
National Place Building, Room 1010
Washington, DC 20530
(202) 616-0521 voice
(202) 616-1717 fax
Attn: Mr. Joseph K. Bryan, Director, OSDBU

DEPARTMENT OF LABOR
200 Constitution Ave., N.W.
Rm. C-2318
Washington, DC 20210
(202) 219-9148 voice
(202) 219-9167 fax
Attn: Ms. June Robinson, Director, OSDBU

DEPARTMENT OF STATE
Office of Small and Disadvantaged Business Utilization
Room 633, SA 6
Washington, DC 20522-0602
(703) 875-6824 voice
(703) 875-6825 fax
Attn: Ms. Durie White, Director, OSDBU

DEPARTMENT OF THE AIR FORCE
Office of the Secretary of the Air Force
The Pentagon - Room 5E271
Washington, DC 20330-1060
(703) 697-1950 voice
(703) 614-9266 fax
Attn: Mr. Anthony J. DeLuca, Director, OSDBU (SAF/SB)

DEPARTMENT OF THE ARMY
Office of the Secretary of the Army
106 Army Pentagon
Washington, DC 20310-0106
(703) 697-7753 voice
(703) 693-3898 fax
Attn: Ms. Tracy L. Pinson, Director, OSDBU

DEPARTMENT OF THE INTERIOR
1849 C Street, N.W., Room 2721
Washington, DC 20240
(202) 208-3493 voice
(202) 208-5048 fax
Attn: Mr. Ralph Rausch, Acting Director, OSDBU

DEPARTMENT OF THE NAVY
Office of the Secretary of the Navy
2211 S. Clark Place
Arlington, VA 22244-5102
(703) 602-2700 voice
(703) 602-2477 or 8569 fax
Attn: Mr. Don L. Hathaway, Director, OSDBU

DEPARTMENT OF THE TREASURY
1500 Pennsylvania Avenue, N.W., Room 6100 - Annex
Washington, DC 20220
(202) 622-0530 voice
(202) 622-2273 fax
Attn: Mr. T. J. Garcia, Director, OSDBU

DEPARTMENT OF TRANSPORTATION
400 7th Street, S.W., Room 9414
Washington, DC 20590
(202) 366-1930 voice
(202) 366-7228 fax
Attn: Ms. Luz Hopewell, Director, OSDBU

DEPARTMENT OF VETERANS AFFAIRS
810 Vermont Avenue, N.W. (00SB)
Washington, DC 20420
(202) 565-8124 voice
(202) 565-8156 fax
Attn: Mr. Scott F. Denniston, Director, OSDBU (005SB)

ENVIRONMENTAL PROTECTION AGENCY
401 M Street, S.W., Mail Code 1230C
Washington, DC 20460
(703) 305-7777 voice
(703) 305-6606 fax
Attn: Mr. Leon H. Hampton, Jr., Director, OSDBU

EXECUTIVE OFFICE OF THE PRESIDENT
Office of Administration/General Services
New Executive Office Building
725 17th Street, N.W., Rm. 5001
Washington, DC 20503
(202) 395-3314 voice
(202) 395-3982 fax
Attn: Ms. Thelma Toler, Small Business Specialist

EXPORT-IMPORT BANK OF THE U.S.
811 Vermont Avenue, N.W., Room 1017
Washington, DC 20571
(202) 565-3335 voice
(202) 565-3319 fax
Attn: Mr. Daniel A. Garcia, Administrative Officer

FANNIE MAE
3900 Wisconsin Avenue, N.W.
Washington, DC 20016-2899
(202) 752-6080 voice
(202) 752-3804 fax
Attn: Ms. Marjorie Smith, Director, Minority and Women-Owned Businesses Office of Diversity

FARM CREDIT
ADMINISTRATION
1501 Farm Credit Drive
McLean, VA 22102-5090
(703) 883-4149 voice
(703) 734-5784 fax
Attn: Mr. James Judge, Chief of
Contracting and Procurement

FEDERAL COMMUNICA-
TIONS COMMISSION
1250 23rd Street, N.W., Room 119
Washington, DC 20554
(202) 418-0930 voice
Attn: Ms. Sonna Stampone,
Chief, Acquisitions Branch

FEDERAL DEPOSIT INSUR-
ANCE CORPORATION (FDIC)
Minority and Women-Owned
Business Development Branch
Office of Equal Opportunity
801 17th Street, N.W., Suite 1248
Washington, DC 20429
(202) 416-2489 voice
(202) 416-4454 fax
Attn: Ms. Velda Fludd, MWOB
Specialist

FEDERAL EMERGENCY
MANAGEMENT AGENCY
500 C Street, S.W., Room 350
Washington, DC 20472
(202) 646-3743 voice
(202) 646-3695 fax
Attn: Ms. Christine Makris,
Director, Acquisition Support
Division, Office of Financial
Management

FEDERAL HOUSING FINANCE
BOARD (FHFB)
1777 F Street, N.W., 3rd Floor
Washington, DC 20006
(202) 408-2582 voice
(202) 408-2580 fax
Attn: Mr. Ernest Roane, Contracting Officer

FEDERAL MEDIATION AND
CONCILIATION SERVICE
2100 K Street, N.W., Room 105
Washington, DC 20427
(202) 606-8111 voice
(202) 606-4254 fax
Attn: Mr. Dan Funkhouser, Director of Administration Services

FEDERAL TRADE
COMMISSION
6th and Pennsylvania Avenue,
N.W., Room 706
Washington, DC 20580
(202) 326-2258 or 2257 voice
(202) 326-3529 fax
Attn: Ms. Jean Sefchick, Chief of
Procurement

FREDDIE MAC
7900 W. Park Drive,
MAILSTOP 919
McLean, VA 22102
(703) 905-5329 voice
(703) 905-5403 fax
Attn: Mr. Jay Inouye, Manager,
Supplier Diversity

GENERAL SERVICES
ADMINISTRATION
18th and F Streets, N.W., Room 6029
Washington, DC 20405
(202) 501-1021 voice
(202) 208-5938 fax
Attn: Mr. Robert L. Neal, Jr., Associate Administrator, Office of Enterprise Development

INTERNATIONAL TRADE COMMISSION
500 E Street, S.W., Room 214
Washington, DC 20436
(202) 205-2730 voice
(202) 205-2150 fax
Attn: Ms. Myra Lay, Purchasing Agent
        Mr. Michael Boling, Acting Chief of Procurement

LIBRARY OF CONGRESS
Office of Contracts and Logistics
1701 Brightseat Road
Landover, MD 20785
(202) 707-0412 voice
(202) 707-8611 fax
Attn: Mr. Napoleon Jasper, Procurement Policy Administrator

NATIONAL AERONAUTICS AND SPACE ADMINISTRATION
NASA Headquarters, Mail Code K, Room 9K70
300 E Street, S.W.
Washington, DC 20546-0001
(202) 358-2088 voice
(202) 358-3261 fax
Attn: Mr. Ralph C. Thomas, III, Associate Administrator, OSDBU

NATIONAL ARCHIVES AND RECORDS ADMINISTRATION
8601 Adelphi Road, Room 4400
College Park, MD 20740-6001
(301) 713-6755 voice
(301) 713-6910 fax
Attn: Ms. Joyce Murray, Contracting Officer, Acquisition Services Division ADM.ACQ

NATIONAL CREDIT UNION ADMINISTRATION
Office of Administration
1775 Duke Street
Alexandria, VA 22314-3428
(703) 518-6410 voice
(703) 518-6433 fax
Attn: Ms. Sharon Holeman, Contracting Officer

NATIONAL LABOR RELATIONS BOARD
1099 14th Street, N.W., Suite 6100
Washington, DC 20570
(202) 273-4210 voice
(202) 273-2849 fax
Attn: Ms. Linda Blake, Procurement Specialist, or Ms. Paula Roy, Chief of Contracting and Procurement Section

NATIONAL SCIENCE
FOUNDATION
4201 Wilson Blvd., Room 590
Arlington, VA 22230
(703) 306-1390 voice
(703) 306-0337 fax
Attn: Dr. Donald Senich, Director,
OSDBU

NUCLEAR REGULATORY
COMMISSION
Office of Small Business and
Civil Rights
Mail Stop T-2F18
Washington, DC 20555
(301) 415-7380 voice
(301) 415-5953 fax
Attn: Mr. Vandy Miller, Director, Office of Small Business and
Civil Rights

OFFICE OF PERSONNEL
MANAGEMENT
Contracting Division
1900 E Street, N.W., Room SB427
Washington, DC 20415
(202) 606-2240 voice
(202) 606-1464 fax
Attn: Ms. Vivian Bethea, Small
Business Technical Advisor

OFFICE OF THE COMPTROL-
LER OF THE CURRENCY (OCC)
Acquisitions and Procurement
Branch
250 E Street, S.W., Mail Stop 4-13
Washington, DC 20219
(202) 874-5040 voice
(202) 874-5625 fax
Attn: Vacant, Contract Specialist

OFFICE OF THRIFT SUPERVI-
SION
Department of the Treasury
1700 G Street, N.W., 3rd Floor
Washington, DC 20552
(202) 906-7624 voice
(202) 906-5748 fax
Attn: Mr. Douglas Mason,
Senior Contract Specialist and
Advocate, Outreach Program

PENNSYLVANIA AVENUE
DEVELOPMENT
CORPORATION
1331 Pennsylvania Avenue,
N.W., Suite 1220 North
Washington, DC 20004-1703
(202) 724-0761 voice
(202) 724-0246 fax
Attn: Ms. Susan Zusy, Affirma-
tive Action Project Manager

RAILROAD RETIREMENT
BOARD
Bureau of Supply and Service
844 North Rush Street, Rm. 1230
Chicago, IL 60611
(312) 751-4565 voice
(312) 751-4923 fax
Attn: Mr. Henry Valiulis, Director

RESOLUTION TRUST
CORPORATION (RTC)
801 17th Street, N.W., Room 1201
Washington, DC 20434
(202) 416-6925 voice
(202) 416-2466 fax
Attn: Ms. Johnnie B. Booker, Director, Office of Equal Opportunity

SMALL BUSINESS ADMINIS-
TRATION
Director, Office of Procurement
and Grants Management
409 Third Street, S.W., 5th floor
Washington, DC 20416
(202) 205-6622 voice
(202) 205-6821 fax
Attn: Sharon Gurley, Director

SMITHSONIAN INSTITUTION
Office of Equal Employment and
Minority Affairs SDBU Program
915 L'Enfant Plaza, S.W.
Washington, DC 20560
(202) 287-3508 voice
(202) 287-3492 fax
Attn: Mr. Mauricio P. Vera, Small
and Disadvantaged Business
Utilization Program Manager

SURFACE TRANSPORTATION
BOARD (formerly the INTER-
STATE COMMERCE COMMIS-
SION)
Surface Transportation Board
contracts are processed through
the DEPARTMENT OF TRANS-
PORTATION

TENNESSEE VALLEY
AUTHORITY
1101 Market Street, EB2B-C
Chattanooga, TN 37402-2801
(423) 751-6269 voice
(423) 751-6890 fax
Attn: Mr. George Provost, Manager,
OSDBU

UNITED STATES INFORMA-
TION AGENCY
400 6th St., S.W., Room 1725
Washington, DC 20547
(202) 205-5404 voice
(202) 401-2410 fax
Attn: Ms. Georgia Hubert,
Director, OSDBU

UNITED STATES POSTAL
SERVICE
475 L'Enfant Plaza, S.W., Rm. 3821
Washington, DC 20260-5616
(202) 268-6578 or 268-6566 voice
(202) 268-6573 fax
Attn: Mr. Richard J. Hernandez,
Manager, Supplier Diversity

[1]   Small Business Administration:
http://www.sbaonline.sba.gov/gopher/Local-Information/Business-Information-
Centers/

SOME
ORGANIZATIONS
THAT PROMOTE
SMALL AND DISADVANTAGED
BUSINESS INTERESTS

APPENDIX III

American Association of Black
Women Entrepreneurs
815 Thayer Ave., Suite 1628
Silver Spring, MD 20911-3853
(301) 585-8051

Asian American Business
Roundtable[1]
11228 Georgia Ave., No. 9
Wheaton, MD 20902
(301) 946-4516

Asian Business Association
1041 S. Lower Asuza Road
El Monte, CA 91731
(818) 452-1242

Latin American Management
Association
419 New Jersey Ave., SE
Washington, DC 20003
(202) 546-3803

Minority Organizations: A
National Directory
Garrett Park Press
P.O. Box 190E
Garrett Park, MD 20896
(301) 946-2553

Minority Business Development
Agency
U.S. Department of Commerce
14th and Constitution Ave., NW
Washington, DC 20230
(202) 482-3163

National Association of
Minority Contractors
1333 F St., NW, Suite 500
Washington, DC 20004
(202) 347-8259

National Association of
Minority Enterprises
National Press Building
Suite 1060-B
Washington, DC 20045
(202) 347-2467

National Association of
Purchasing Management
P.O. Box 22160
Tempe, AZ 85285-2160
(800) 888-6276

National Center for American
Indian Enterprise Development
953 E. Juanita Ave.
Mesa, AZ 85204
(602) 831-7524

National Minority Business
Council
235 E. 42nd St.
New York, NY 10017
(212) 573-2385

National Minority Supplier
Development Council, Inc.
15 W. 39th St., 9th Floor
New York, NY 10018
(212) 944-2430

NISH
2235 Cedar Lane
Vienna, VA 22182
(703) 641-2704

Small Business Administration
Procurement Automated Source
System
Mail Code 6256
Washington, DC 20416
(800) 231-PASS

Try Us Resources, Inc.
2105 Central Ave., NE
Minneapolis. MN 55418
(612) 781-6819

U.S. Hispanic Chamber of
Commerce
1030 15th St., NW., Suite 206
Washington, DC 20005
(202) 841-1212

[1] *N.A.P.M. Insights*,
November 1994, page 52.

FOREIGN EMBASSIES LOCATED IN THE UNITED STATES

APPENDIX IV

This information was gathered from the U.S. State Department in Washington, D.C.

AFGHANISTAN
Embassy of the Republic of
Afghanistan
2341 Wyoming Avenue, N.W.
Washington, DC 20008
(202) 234-3770 voice
(202) 328-3516 fax

ALBANIA
Embassy of the Republic of
Albania
1511 K Street, N.W., Suite 1010
Washington, DC 20005
(202) 223-4942 voice
(202) 628-7342 fax

ALGERIA
Embassy of the Democratic and
Popular Republic of Algeria
2118 Kalaroma Road, N.W.
Washington, DC 20008
(202) 265-2800 voice

ANGOLA
Embassy of the Republic of
Angola
1819 L Street, N.W.
Washington, DC 20036
(202) 785-1156 voice
(202) 785-1258 fax

ANTIGUA/BARBUDA
Embassy of Antigua and
Barbuda
3216 New Mexico Ave., N.W.,
Suite 400
Washington, DC 20036
(202) 362-5122 voice
(202) 362-5225 fax

ARGENTINA
Embassy of the Argentine
Republic
1600 New Hampshire Ave., N.W.
Washington, DC 20009
(202) 939-6400 voice

AUSTRALIA
Embassy of Australia
1601 Massachusetts Ave., N.W.
Washington, DC 20036
(202) 797-3000 voice
(202) 797-3168 fax
http://www.aust.emb.nw.dc.us

AUSTRIA
Embassy of Austria
3524 International Court, N.W.
Washington, DC 20008
(202) 895-6700 voice
(202) 895-6750 fax
http://www.austria.org/web/
austria/

AZERBAIJAN
Embassy of the Republic of
Azerbaijan
927 - 15th St., N.W., Suite 700
Washington, DC 20005
(202) 842-0001 voice
(202) 842-0004 fax

BAHAMAS
Embassy of the Commonwealth
of the Bahamas
2220 Massachusetts Avenue, N.W.
Washington, DC 20008
(202) 319-2660 voice
(202) 319-2668 fax

BAHRAIN
Embassy of the State of Bahrain
3502 International Drive, N.W.
Washington, DC 20008
(202) 342-0741 voice
(202) 362-2192 fax

BANGLADESH
Embassy of the People's Republic of Bangladesh
2201 Wisconsin Avenue, N.W.
Washington, DC 20007
(202) 342-8372 voice

BARBADOS
Embassy of the Barbados
2144 Wyoming Avenue, N.W.
Washington, DC 20008
(202) 939-9200 voice
(202) 332-7467 fax

BELARUS
Embassy of the Republic of
Belarus
1619 New Hampshire Avenue,
N.W.
Washington, DC 20009
(202) 986-1604 voice
(202) 986-1605 fax

BELGIUM
Embassy of Belgium
3330 Garfield Street, N.W.
Washington, DC 20008
(202) 333-6900 voice
(202) 333-3079 fax

BELIZE
Embassy of Belize
2535 Massachusetts Ave., N.W.
Washington, DC 20008
(202) 332-9636 voice
(202) 332-6888 fax

BENIN
Embassy of the Republic of Benin
2737 Cathedral Avenue, N.W.
Washington, DC 20008
(202) 232-6656 voice
(202) 265-1996 fax

BOLIVIA
Embassy of the Republic of
Bolivia
3014 Massachusetts Ave., N.W.
Washington, DC 20008
(202) 483-4410 voice
(202) 328-3712 fax

BOSNIA AND HERZEGOVINA
Embassy of the Republic of
Bosnia and Herzegovina
1707 L Street, N.W., Suite 760
Washington, DC 20036
(202) 833-3612 voice
(202) 833-2061 fax

BOTSWANA
Embassy of the Republic of
Botswana
3400 International Drive, N.W.,
Suite 7M
Washington, DC 20008
(202) 244-4990 voice
(202) 244-4164 fax

BRAZIL
Brazilian Embassy
3006 Massachusetts Ave., N.W.
Washington, DC 20008
(202) 745-2700 voice
(202) 745-2827 fax

BRUNEI
Embassy of the State of Brunei
Darussalam
Watergate, 2600 Virginia Ave.,
N.W. Suite 300, Third Floor
Washington, DC 20037
(202) 342-0159 voice
(202) 342-0158 fax

BULGARIA
Embassy of the Republic of
Bulgaria
1621 - 22nd St., N.W.
Washington, DC 20008
(202) 387-7969 voice
(202) 234-7973 fax

BURKINA FASO
Embassy of Burkina Faso
2340 Massachusetts Ave., N.W.
Washington, DC 20008
(202) 332-5577 voice

BURMA (see MYANMAR)

BURUNDI
Embassy of the Republic of Burundi
2233 Wisconsin Ave., N.W., Ste. 212
Washington, DC 20007
(202) 342-2574 voice

CAMBODIA
Royal Embassy of Cambodia
4500 - 16th Street, N.W.
Washington, DC 20011
(202) 726-7742 voice
(202) 726-8381 fax

CAMEROON
Embassy of the Republic of Cameroon
2349 Massachusetts Ave., N.W.
Washington, DC 20008
(202) 265-8790 voice

CANADA
Embassy of Canada
501 Pennsylvania Avenue, N.W.
Washington, DC 20001
(202) 682-1740 voice
(202) 682-7726 fax
http://www.nstn.ca/wshdc/

CAPE VERDE
Embassy of the Republic of Cape Verde
3415 Massachusetts Ave., N.W.
Washington, DC 20007
(202) 965-6820 voice
(202) 965-1207 fax

CENTRAL AFRICAN REPUBLIC
Embassy of the Central African Republic
1618 - 22nd Street, N.W.
Washington, DC 20008
(202) 483-7800 voice
(202) 332-9893 fax

CHAD
Embassy of the Republic of Chad
2002 R Street, N.W.
Washington, DC 20009
(202) 462-4009 voice
(202) 265-1937 fax

CHILE
Embassy of Chile
1732 Massachusetts Ave., N.W.
Washington, DC 20036
(202) 785-1746 voice
(202) 887-5579 fax

CHINA
Embassy of the People's
Republic of China
2300 Connecticut Avenue, N.W.
Washington, DC 20008
(202) 328-2500 voice

COLOMBIA
Embassy of Colombia
2118 Leroy Place, N.W.
Washington, DC 20008
(202) 387-8338 voice
(202) 232-8643 fax

COMOROS
Embassy of the Federal and
Islamic Republic of the Comoros
c/o Permanent Mission of the
Federal and Islamic Republic of
the Comoros
336 East 45th Street, Second Floor
New York, N.Y. 10017

CONGO
Embassy of the Republic of the
Congo
4891 Colorado Avenue, N.W.
Washington, DC 20011
(202) 726-0825 voice
(202) 726-1860 fax

COSTA RICA
Embassy of Costa Rica
2114 S. Street, N.W.
Washington, DC 20008
(202) 234-2945 voice
(202) 265-4795 fax

COTE D'IVOIRE (Ivory Coast)
Embassy of the Republic of Cote
D'Ivoire
2424 Massachusetts Ave., N.W.
Washington, DC 20008
(202) 797-0300 voice

CROATIA
Embassy of the Republic of
Croatia
2343 Massachusetts Ave., N.W.
Washington, DC 20008
(202) 588-5899 voice
(202) 588-8936 fax

CYPRUS
Embassy of the Republic of
Cyprus
2211 R Street, N.W.
Washington, DC 20008
(202) 462-5772 voice

CZECH
Embassy of the Czech Republic
3900 Spring of Freedom St., N.W.
Washington, DC 20008
(202) 363-6315 voice
(202) 966-8540 fax
http://www.czech.cz/washington/

DENMARK
Royal Danish Embassy
3200 Whitehaven Street, N.W.
Washington, DC 20008
(202) 234-4300 voice
(202) 328-1470 fax

DIJIBOUTI
Embassy of the Republic of
Dijibouti
1156 - 15th Street, N.W., Ste. 515
Washington, DC 20005
(202) 331-0270 voice
(202) 331-0302 fax

DOMINICA
Embassy of the Commonwealth
of Dominica
316 New Mexico Avenue, N.W.
Washington, DC 20016
(202) 364-6781 voice
(202) 364-6791 fax

DOMINICAN REPUBLIC
Embassy of the Dominican
Republic
1715 - 22nd Street, N.W.
Washington, DC 20008
(202) 332-6280 voice
(202) 265-8057 fax

ECUADOR
Embassy of Ecuador
2535 - 15th Street., N.W.
Washington, DC 20009
(202) 234-7200 voice

EGYPT
Embassy of the Arab Republic of
Egypt
3521 International Court, N.W.
Washington, DC 20008
(202) 895-5400 voice
(202) 244-4319 fax

EL SALVADOR
Embassy of El Salvador
2308 California Street, N.W.
Washington, DC 20008
(202) 265-9671 voice

EQUATORIAL GUINEA
Embassy of Equitorial Guinea
c/o 57 Magnolia Avenue
Mount Vernon, N.Y. 10553
(914) 738-9584 voice

ERITEA
Embassy of the State of Eritea
910 - 17th Street, N.W., Suite 400
Washington, DC 20006
(202) 429-1991 voice
(202) 429-9004 fax

ESTONIA
Embassy of Estonia
2131 Massachusetts Ave., N.W.
Washington, DC 20008
(202) 588-0101 voice
(202) 588-0108 fax

ETHIOPIA
Embassy of Ethiopia
2134 Kalorama Road, N.W.
Washington, DC 20008
(202) 234-2281 voice
(202) 328-7950 fax

EUROPEAN UNION
Delegation of the European
Commission
2300 M Street, N.W.
Washington, DC 20037
(202) 862-9500 voice
(202) 429-1766 fax

FIJI
Embassy of the Republic of Fiji
2233 Wisconsin Ave., N.W., Ste. 240
Washington, DC 20007
(202) 337-8320 voice
(202) 337-1996 fax

FINLAND
Embassy of Finland
3301 Massachusetts Ave., N.W.
Washington, DC 20008
(202) 298-5800 voice
(202) 298-6030 fax
http://www.finnemb.nw.dc.us/
web/finland/index.html

FRANCE
Embassy of France
4101 Reservoir Road, N.W.
Washington, DC 20007
(202) 944-6000 voice
http://www.info-france.org/
intheus/embassyw.html

GABON
Embassy of the Gabonese Republic
2034 - 20th Street, N.W., Ste. 200
Washington, DC 20009
(202) 797-1100 voice
(202) 332-0668 fax

THE GAMBIA
Embassy of The Gambia
1155 - 5th Street, N.W., Suite 1000
Washington, DC 20005
(202) 785-1399 voice
(202) 785-1430 fax

GEORGIA
Embassy of the Republic of Georgia
1511 K Street, N.W., Suite 424
Washington, DC 20005
(202) 393-5959 voice
(202) 393-6060 fax

GERMANY
Embassy of the Federal
Republic of Germany
4645 Reservoir Road, N.W.
Washington, DC 20007
(202) 298-4000 voice
(202) 298-4249 fax

GHANA
Embassy of Ghana
3512 International Drive, N.W.
Washington, DC 20008
(202) 686-4520 voice
(202) 686-4527 fax

GREECE
Embassy of Greece
2221 Massachusetts Avenue
N.W.
Washington, DC 20008
(202) 939-5800 voice
(202) 939-5824 fax

GRENADA
Embassy of Grenada
1701 New Hampshire Avenue,
N.W.
Washington, DC 20009
(202) 265-2561 voice

GUATEMALA
Embassy of Guatemala
2220 R Street, N.W.
Washington, DC 20008
(202) 745-4952 voice
(202) 745-1908 fax

GUINEA
Embassy of the Republic of
Guinea
2112 Leroy Place, N.W.
Washington, DC 20009
(202) 483-9420 voice
(202) 483-8688 fax

GUINEA-BISSAU
Embassy of the Republic of
Guinea-Bissau
918 - 16th Street, N.W., Mezza-
nine Suite
Washington, DC 20006
(202) 872-4222 voice

GUYANA
2490 Tracy Place, N.W.
Washington, DC 20008
(202) 265-6900 voice

HAITI
Embassy of the Republic of Haiti
2311 Massachusetts Ave., N.W.
Washington, DC 20008
(202) 332-4090 voice
(202) 745-7215 fax

THE HOLY SEE (Vatican)
Apostolic Nunciature
3339 Massachusetts Ave., N.W.
Washington, DC 20008
(202) 333-7121 voice

HONDURAS
Embassy of Honduras
3007 Tilden Street, N.W.
Washington, DC 20008
(202) 966-7702 voice
(202) 966-9751 fax

HUNGARY
Embassy of the Republic of
Hungary
3910 Shoemaker Street, N.W.
Washington, DC 20008
(202) 362-6730 voice
(202) 966-8135 fax

ICELAND
Embassy of Iceland
1156 - 15th St., N.W., Ste. 1200
Washington, DC 20005
(202) 265-6653 voice
(202) 265-6656 fax
http://www.iceland.org

INDIA
Embassy of India
2107 Massachusetts Ave., N.W.
Washington, DC 20008
(202) 939-7000 voice

INDONESIA
Embassy of the Republic of
Indonesia
2020 Massachusetts Ave., N.W.
Washington, DC 20008
(202) 775-5200 voice
(202) 775-5365 fax

IRELAND
Embassy of Ireland
2234 Massachusetts Ave., N.W.
Washington, DC 20008
(202) 462-3939 voice

ISRAEL
Embassy of Israel
3514 International Drive, N.W.
Washington, DC 20008
(202) 364-5500 voice
(202) 364-5610 fax
http://www.israelemb.org

ITALY
Embassy of Italy
1601 Fuller Street, N.W.
Washington, DC 20009
(202) 328-5500 voice
(202) 483-2187 fax
http://www.italyemb.nw.dc.us/
italy/index.html

JAMAICA
Embassy of Jamaica
1520 New Hampshire Ave., N.W.
Washington, DC 20036
(202) 452-0660 voice
(202) 452-0081 fax

JAPAN
Embassy of Japan
2520 Massachusetts Ave., N.W.
Washington, DC 20008
(202) 939-6700 voice
(202) 328-2187 fax

JORDAN
Embassy of the Hashemite
Kingdom of Jordan
3504 International Drive, N.W.
Washington, DC 20008
(202) 966-2664 voice
(202) 966-3110 fax

KAZAKHSTAN
Embassy of the Republic of
Kazakhstan
3421 Massachusetts Ave., N.W.
Washington, DC 20008
(202) 333-4504 voice

KENYA
Embassy of the Republic of
Kenya
2249 R Street, N.W.
Washington, DC 20008
(202) 387-6101 voice
(202) 462-3829 fax

KOREA
Embassy of Korea
2450 Massachusetts Ave., N.W.
Washington, DC 20008
(202) 524-9273 voice

KUWAIT
Embassy of the State of Kuwait
2940 Tilden Street, N.W.
Washington, DC 20008
(202) 966-0702 voice
(202) 966-0517 fax

KYRGYSTAN
Embassy of the Kyrgyz Republic
1511 K Street, N.W., Suite 706
Washington, DC 20005
(202) 347-3732 voice
(202) 347-3718 fax

LAOS
Embassy of the Lao People's
Democratic Republic
222 S Street, N.W.
Washington, DC 20008
(202) 332-6416 voice
(202) 332-4923 fax

LATVIA
Embassy of Latvia
4325 - 17th Street, N.W.
Washington, DC 20011
(202) 726-8213 voice
(202) 726-6785 fax

LEBANON
Embassy of Lebanon
2560 - 28th Street, N.W.
Washington, DC 20008
(202) 939-6300 voice
(202) 939-6324 fax

LESOTHO
Embassy of the Kingdom of
Lesotho
2511 Massachusetts Ave., N.W.
Washington, DC 20008
(202) 797-5533 voice
(202) 234-6815 fax

LIBERIA
Embassy of the Republic of
Liberia
5201 - 16th Street, N.W.
Washington, DC 20011
(202) 723-0437 voice

LITHUANIA
Embassy of the Republic of
Lithuania
2622 - 16th Street, N.W.
Washington, DC 20009
(202) 234-5860 voice
(202) 328-0466 fax

LUXEMBOURG
Embassy of the Grand Duchy of
Luxembourg
2200 Massachusetts Ave., N.W.
Washington, DC 20008
(202) 265-4171 voice
(202) 328-8270 fax

MALAYSIA
Embassy of Malaysia
2401 Massachusetts Ave., N.W.
Washington, DC 20008
(202) 328-2700 voice
(202) 483-7661 fax

MALI
Embassy of the Republic of Mali
2130 R Street, N.W.
Washington, DC 20008
(202) 332-2249 voice

MALTA
Embassy of Malta
2017 Connecticut Avenue, N.W.
Washington, DC 20008
(202) 462-3611 voice
(202) 387-5470 fax

MARSHALL ISLANDS
Embassy of the Republic of the
Marshall Islands
2433 Massachusetts Ave., N.W.
Washington, DC 20008
(202) 234-5414 voice
(202) 232-3236 fax

MAURITANIA
Embassy of the Islamic Republic
of Mauritania
2129 Leroy Place, N.W.
Washington, DC 20008
(202) 232-5700 voice

MAURITIUS
Embassy of the Republic of
Mauritius
4301 Connecticut Ave., N.W., Ste. 441
Washington, DC 20008
(202) 244-1491 voice
(202) 966-0983 fax

MEXICO
Embassy of Mexico
1911 Pennsylvania Ave., N.W.
Washington, DC 20006
(202) 728-1600 voice

MICRONESIA
Embassy of the Federal States of
Micronesia
1725 N Street, N.W.
Washington, DC 20036
(202) 223-4383 voice
(202) 223-4391 fax

MOLDOVA
Embassy of the Republic of
Moldova
1511 K Street, N.W., Stes. 329, 333
Washington, DC 20005
(202) 783-3012 voice
(202) 783-3342 fax

MONGOLIA
Embassy of Mongolia
2833 M Street, N.W.
Washington, DC 20007
(202) 333-7117 voice
(202) 298-9227 fax

MOROCCO
Embassy of the Kingdom of
Morocco
1601 - 21st Street, N.W.
Washington, DC 20009
(202) 462-7979 voice
(202) 265-0161 fax

MOZAMBIQUE
Embassy of the Republic of
Mozambique
1990 M Street, N.W., Suite 570
Washington, DC 20036
(202) 293-7146 voice
(202) 835-0245 fax

MYNAMAR
Embassy of the Union of
Mynamar
2300 S Street, N.W.
Washington, DC 20008
(202) 332-9044 voice

NAMIBIA
Embassy of the Republic of
Namibia
1605 New Hampshire Ave., N.W.
Washington, DC 20009
(202) 986-0540 voice
(202) 986-0443 fax

NETHERLANDS
Kingdom of the Netherlands
Royal Netherlands Embassy
4200 Wisconsin Avenue, N.W.
Washington, DC 20016
(202) 244-5300 voice
(202) 362-3430 fax

NEW ZEALAND
Embassy of New Zealand
37 Observatory Circle, N.W.
Washington, DC 20008
(202) 328-4800 voice

NICARAGUA
Embassy of Nicaragua
1627 New Hampshire Ave., N.W.
Washington, DC 20009
(202) 939-6570 voice

NIGER
Embassy of the Republic of Niger
2204 R Street, N.W.
Washington, DC 20008
(202) 483-4224 voice

NIGERIA
Embassy of the Federal Republic of Nigeria
1333 - 16th Street, N.W.
Washington, DC 20036
(202) 986-4400 voice

NORWAY
Royal Norwegian Embassy
2720 - 34th Street, N.W.
Washington, DC 20008
(202) 333-6000 voice
(202) 337-0870 fax
http://www.norway.org/

OMAN
Embassy of the Sultanate of Oman
2535 Belmont Road, N.W.
Washington, DC 20008
(202) 387-1980 voice
(202) 745-4933 fax

PAKISTAN
Embassy of Pakistan
2315 Massachusetts Ave., N.W.
Washington, DC 20008
(202) 939-6200 voice
(202) 387-0484 fax

PALAU
Embassy of the Republic of Palau
444 North Capital Street, N.W.
Washington, DC 20001
(202) 483-1407 voice
(202) 624-7795 fax

PANAMA
Embassy of the Republic of Panama
2862 McGill Terrace, N.W.
Washington, DC 20001
(202) 483-1407 voice

PAPUA NEW GUINEA
Embassy of Papua New Guinea
1615 New Hampshire, N.W.,
Third Floor
Washington, DC 20009
(202) 745-3860 voice
(202) 745-3679 fax

PARAGUAY
Embassy of Paraguay
2400 Massachusetts Ave., N.W.
Washington, DC 20008
(202) 483-6960 voice
(202) 234-4508 fax

PERU
Embassy of Peru
1700 Massachusetts Ave., N.W.
Washington, DC 20036
(202) 833-9860 voice
(202) 659-8124 fax

PHILIPPINES
Embassy of the Philippines
1600 Massachusetts Ave., N.W.
Washington, DC 20036
(202) 467-9300 voice
(202) 328-7614 fax

POLAND
Embassy of the Republic of
Poland
2640 - 16th Street, N.W.
Washington, DC 20009
(202) 234-3800 voice
(202) 328-6271 fax

PORTUGAL
Embassy of Portugal
2125 Kalorama Road, N.W.
Washington, DC 20008
(202) 328-8610 voice
(202) 462-3726 fax

QATAR
Embassy of the State of Qatar
600 New Hampshire Ave., N.W.
Suite 1180
Washington, DC 20036
(202) 338-0111 voice

ROMANIA
Embassy of Romania
1607 - 23rd Street, N.W.
Washington, DC 20008
(202) 332-4846 voice
(202) 232-4748 fax
http://www.embassy.org/
romania/

RUSSIA
Embassy of the Russian
Federation
2650 Wisconsin Avenue, N.W.
Washington, DC 20008
(202) 298-5700 voice
(202) 298-5735 fax

RWANDA
Embassy of the Republic of
Rwanda
1714 New Hampshire Ave., N.W.
Washington, DC 20009
(202) 232-2882 voice
(202) 232-4544 fax

SAINT KITTS AND NEVIS
Embassy of St. Kitts and Nevis
3216 New Mexico Avenue, N.W.
Washington, DC 20016
(202) 686-2636 voice
(202) 686-5740 fax

SAINT LUCIA
Embassy of Saint Lucia
3216 New Mexico Avenue, N.W.
Washington, DC 20016
(202) 364-6792 voice
(202) 364-6728 fax

SAINT VINCENT AND THE
GRENADINES
Saint Vincent and the Grenadines
1717 Massachusetts Ave., N.W., #102
Washington, DC 20036
(202) 462-7806 voice
(202) 462-7807 fax

SAUDI ARABIA
Embassy of Saudi Arabia
601 New Hampshire Ave., N.W.
Washington, DC 20037
(202) 342-3800 voice

SENEGAL
Embassy of the Republic of
Senegal
2112 Wyoming Avenue, N.W.
Washington, DC 20008
(202) 234-0540 voice

SEYCHELLES
Embassy of the Republic of
Seychelles
c/o Permanent Mission of
Seychelles to the United Nations
820 Second Avenue
New York, NY 10017
(212) 687-9766 voice
(212) 922-9177 fax

SIERRA LEONE
Embassy of Sierra Leone
1701 - 19th Street, N.W.
Washington, DC 20009
(202) 939-9261 voice

SINGAPORE
Embassy of the Republic of
Singapore
3501 International Place, N.W.
Washington, DC 20008
(202) 537-3100, (202)537-0876
voice

SLOVAKIA
Embassy of the Slovak Republic
2201 Wisconsin Ave., N.W., Ste. 380
Washington, DC 20007
(202) 965-5161 voice
(202) 965-5166 fax

SLOVENIA
Embassy of the Republic of
Slovenia
1525 New Hampshire Ave., N.W.
Washington, DC 20036
(202) 667-5363 voice
(202) 667-4563 fax

SOUTH AFRICA
Embassy of the Republic of South
Africa
3051 Massachusetts Ave., N.W.
Washington, DC 20008
(202) 232-4400 voice
(202) 265-1607 fax
http://www.southafrica.net

SPAIN
Embassy of Spain
2375 Pennsylvania Ave., N.W.
Washington, DC 20037
(202) 452-0100 voice
(202) 833-5670 fax

SRI LANKA
Embassy of the Democratic
Socialist Republic of Sri Lanka
2148 Wyoming Ave., N.W.
Washington, DC 20008
(202) 483-4025 voice
(202) 232-7181 fax
http://wheat.symgrp.com/
symgrp/srilanka/

SUDAN
Embassy of the Republic of the
Sudan
2210 Massachusetts Av.e, N.W.
Washington, DC 20008
(202) 338-8565 voice
(202) 667-2406 fax

SURINAME
Embassy of the Republic of
Suriname
4301 Connecticut Ave., N.W.,
Suite 108
Washington, DC 20008
(202) 244-7488 voice
(202) 244-5878 fax

SWAZILAND
Embassy of the Kingdom of
Swaziland
3400 International Drive, N.W.
Washington, DC 20008
(202) 362-6683 voice
(202) 244-8059 fax

SWEDEN
Embassy of Sweden
1501 M Street, N.W.
Washington, DC 20005
(202) 467-2600 voice
(202) 467-2699 fax

SWITZERLAND
Embassy of Switzerland
2900 Cathedral Avenue, N.W.
Washington, DC 20008
(202) 745-7900 voice
(202) 387-2564 fax

SYRIA
Embassy of the Syrian Arab
Republic
2215 Wyoming Avenue, N.W.
Washington, DC 20008
(202) 232-6313 voice
(202) 234-9548 fax

TANZANIA
Embassy of the United Republic of
Tanzania
2139 R Street, N.W.
Washington, DC 20008
(202) 939-6125 voice
(202) 797-7408 fax

THAILAND
Embassy of Thailand
1024 Wisconsin Avenue, N.W.
Washington, DC 20007
(202) 944-3600 voice
(202) 944-3611 fax

TOGO
Embassy of the Republic of Togo
2208 Massachusetts Ave., N.W.
Washington, DC 20008
(202) 234-4212 voice
(202) 232-3190 fax

TONGA
Embassy of the Kingdom of
Tonga
1708 Massachusetts Ave., N.W.
Washington, DC 20036
(202) 467-6490 voice

TRINIDAD AND TOBAGO
Embassy of the Republic of
Trinidad and Tobago
1708 Massachusetts Ave., N.W.
Washington, DC 20036
(202) 467-6490 voice
(202) 785-3130 fax

TUNISIA
Embassy of Tunisia
1515 Massachusetts Ave., N.W.
Washington, DC 20005
(202) 862-1850 voice

TURKEY
Embassy of the Republic of Turkey
1714 Massachusetts Ave., N.W.
Washington, DC 20036
(202) 659-8200 voice

TURKMENISTAN
Embassy of Turkmenistan
1511 K Street, N.W., Suite 412
Washington, DC 20008
(202) 737-4800 voice
(202) 737-1152 fax
http://www.infi.net/~embassy/

UGANDA
Embassy of the Republic of
Uganda
5911 - 16th Street, N.W.
Washington, DC 20011
(202) 726-7100 voice
(202) 726-1727 fax

UKRAINE
Embassy of Ukraine
3350 M Street, N.W.
Washington, DC 20007
(202) 333-0606 voice
(202) 333-0817 fax

UNITED ARAB EMIRATES
Embassy of the United Arab
Emirates
3000 K Street, N.W., Suite 600
Washington, DC 20007
(202) 338-6500 voice

UNITED KINGDOM OF GREAT
BRITAIN AND NORTHERN
IRELAND
British Embassy
3100 Massachusetts Ave., N.W.
Washington, DC 20008
(202) 462-1340 voice
(202) 898-4255 fax

URUGUAY
Embassy of Uruguay
1918 F Street, N.W.
Washington, DC 20006
(202) 331-1313
http://www.embassy.org/
uruguay/

UZBEKISTAN
Embassy of the Republic of
Uzbekistan
1511 K Street, N.W., Suite 619
Washington, DC 20005
(202) 638-4266 voice
(202) 638-4268 fax
http://ourworld.compuserve.com/
homepages/Uzbeks/

VENEZUELA
Embassy of the Republic of
Venezuela
1099 - 30th Street, N.W.
Washington, DC 20007
(202) 342-2214 voice

VIETNAM
Liaison Office of the Socialist
Republic of Vietnam
1233 - 20th Street, N.W., Ste. 501
Washington, DC 20036
(202) 861-0737 voice
(202) 861-0917 fax

WESTERN SAMOA
Embassy of Western Samoa
820 Second Avenue, Suite 800
New York, NY 10017
(212) 599-6196 voice
(212) 599-0797 fax

YEMEN
Embassy of the Republic of
Yemen
2600 Virginia Ave., N.W., Ste. 705
Washington, DC 20037
(202) 965-4760 voice
(202) 337-2017 fax

YUGOSLAVIA
Embassy of the former Socialist
Federal Republic of Yugoslavia
2410 California Street, N.W.
Washington, DC 20008
(202) 462-6566 voice

ZAIRE
Embassy of the Republic of Zaire
1800 New Hampshire Ave., N.W.
Washington, DC 20009
(202) 234-7690 voice

ZAMBIA
Embassy of the Republic of Zambia
2419 Massachusetts Ave., N.W.
Washington, DC 20008
(202) 265-9717 voice
(202) 332-0826 fax

ZIMBABWE
Embassy of the Republic of Zimbabwe
1608 New Hampshire Ave., N.W.
Washington, DC 20009
(202) 332-7100 voice
(202) 483-9326 fax

SELECTED
DIRECTORIES,
GUIDES AND SERVICES
FOR BUSINESS CONTACTS,
TRADE ASSOCIATIONS
AND GOVERNMENTS OF THE
EUROPEAN UNION

APPENDIX V

This information was provided by Jonathan Spence of the European Union Delegation of the European Commission, 2300 M Street NW, Washington, D.C. 20037
(202) 862-9500.

Reference Books

*   Available online
\#   Available on CD-ROM

*ABC Europ Production
ABC Publishing Group
P.O. Box 40 34
W-6100 Darmstadt, Germany
(49 61) 513-8920 voice
(49 61) 513-3164 fax

America's Corporate Families and International Affiliates
ISSN: 0740-4018
Dun and Bradstreet Information Services
3 Sylvan Way
Parsippany, NJ 07054-3896
(201) 605-6000 (800) 234-3867 voice

Corporate Location
ISSN: 1352-3163
Century House Information, Ltd.
22 Towcester Road
Old Stratford, Milton Keynes
Buckinghamshire MK19 6AQ, England
(44 908) 560 555 voice
(44 908) 560 470 fax

*D & B Europa
Dun & Bradstreet, Ltd.
Holmers Farm Way
High Wycombe
Buckinghamshire HP12 4UL, England
(44 494) 422 000 voice
(44 494) 422 260 fax

Directory of American Firms Operating in Foreign Countries
ISSN: 0070-5071
World Trade Academy Press, Inc.
50 East 42nd Street, Suite 509
New York, NY 10017-5480
(212) 697-4999 voice
(212) 949-4001 fax

*#Directory of Corporate Affiliations - International Public and
Private Companies
 ISSN: 0736-9778
National Register Publishing
Reed Reference Publishing Company
121 Chanlon Road, Box 31
New Providence, NJ 07974-9903
(908) 464-6800, (800) 521-8110 voice
(908) 665-6688 fax

Directory of European Community Trade and Professional
Associations
ISSN: 0771-7865
UNIPUB
4611-F Assembly Drive
Lanham, MD 20706-4391
(301) 459-7666, (800) 274-4888 voice
(301) 459-0056 fax

Directory of Foreign Firms Operating in the United States
ISSN: 0070-5543
World Trade Academy Press, Inc.
50 East 42nd Street, Suite 509
New York, NY 10017-5480
(212) 697-4999 voice
(212) 949-4001 fax

#Europages CD-ROM
SEAT - Divisione SpA
Via S. Rita da Cascia 33
20143 Milan, Italy

Europe's 15,000 Largest Companies
ISSN: 0800-0638
E L C Publishing Ltd.
109 Uxbridge Road
Eating, London W5 STL, England
(44 815) 662 288 voice
(44 815) 664 931 fax

Export Documentation
International Trade Institute
5055 North Main Street
Dayton, OH 45415
(513) 276-5995, (800) 543-2453 voice
(513) 276-5920 fax

Export Sales and Marketing Manual
ISSN: 1054-8327
Export USA Publications
4141 Parklawn Avenue South, Suite 110
Minneapolis, MN 55435
(612) 893-0624, (800) 876-0624 voice
(612) 893-1626 fax

Exporters' Encyclopaedia
ISSN: 0732-0159
Dun and Bradstreet, Inc.
3 Sylvan Way
Parsippany, NJ 07054-3896
(201) 605-6000, (800) 234-3867 phone
(201) 605-6911 fax

*#FINDEX: The Worldwide Directory of Market Research Reports,
Studies & Surveys
ISSN: 0273-4125
Cambridge Information Group Directories, Inc.
7200 Wisconsin Avenue
Bethesda, MD 20814
(301) 961-6750, (800) 843-7751 voice
(301) 961-6720 fax

A Guide to Selling Your Service Overseas
Northern California District Export Council
450 Golden Gate Avenue
Box 36013
San Francisco, CA 94102
(415) 433-9084 voice

International Directory of Importers: Europe
ISSN: 1050-5555
Interdata
1741 Kekamek NW
Poulsbo, WA 98370
(360) 779-1511 voice
(360) 697-4696 fax

*#Kompass Belgium
ISSN: 0778-4147
Croner Publications, Inc.
34 Jericho Turnpike
Jericho, NY 11753
(516) 333-9085 FAX (516) 338-4986

Kompass France: Professionnels
66 quai du Marechal Joffre
92415 Courbevoie Cedex, France

Kompass Germany
Croner Publications, Inc.
34 Jericho Turnpike
Jericho, NY 11753
(516) 333-9085 voice
(516) 338-4986 fax

Kompass Holland
ISSN: 0075-6660
Croner Publications, Inc.
34 Jericho Turnpike
Jericho, NY 11753
(516) 333-9085 voice
(516) 338-4986 fax

#Kompass Italy
ISSN: 0075-6687
Kompass Italia S.p.A.
via Seruais, 125
10146 Turin, Italy

Kompass Spain
ISSN: 0075-6644
Croner Publications, Inc.
34 Jericho Turnpike
Jericho, NY 11753
(516) 333-9085 voice
(516) 338-4986 fax

*#Kompass Sweden
ISSN: 0075-6725
Reed Reference Publishing Company
121 Chanlon Road, Box 31
New Providence, NJ 07974-9903
(908) 464-6800, (800) 521-8110 voice
FAX (908) 665-6688

*#Kompass United Kingdom
Kompass
Windsor Court
East Grinstead House
East Grinstead, West Sussex RH10 1XD, England
(44 342) 326 972 voice
(44 342) 335 992 fax

Made in Europe Buyers' Guide
ISSN: 0172-2182
Made in Europe Marketing Organization GmbH
Hahnstr. 70
60528 Frankfurt am Main, Germany
(49 69) 666-8266 voice
(49 69) 666-8276 fax

Mailing Lists of Worldwide Importing Firms
Interdata
1741 Kekamek NW
Poulsbo, WA 98370
(360) 433-3900 voice
(360) 697-4696 fax

Marconi's International Register
ISSN: 0076-4418
Telegraphic Cable & Radio Registrations, Inc.
19 Dogwood Lane, Box 14
Larchmont, NY 10538
(914) 632-8171 voice
(914) 698-1804 fax

*Moody's International Manual
ISSN: 0278-3509
Moody's Investors Service
99 Church Street
New York, NY 10007-0300
(212) 553-0300 voice
(212) 553-4700 fax

*Principal International Businesses: The World Marketing Directory
ISSN: 0097-6288
Dun & Bradstreet International
International Marketing Services
3 Sylvan Way
Parsippany, NJ 07054-3896
(201) 605-6000, (800) 234-3867 voice

*Who Owns Whom: Continental Europe
ISSN: 0083-9302
Dun & Bradstreet, Ltd.
Holmers Farm Way
High Wycombe
Buckinghamshire HP12 4UL, England
(44 494) 422 000 voice
(44 494) 422 260 fax

World Trade Centers Association Directory
World Trade Centers Association
One World Trade Center, Suite 7101
New York, NY 10048
(212) 432-2626 voice
(212) 488-0064 fax

#Worldtariff Customs Tariff Guidebooks
Worldtariff
220 Montgomery Street, Suite 432
San Francisco, CA 94104
(415) 391-7501 voice
(415) 391-7537 fax

#Yearbook of International Organizations
ISSN: 0084-3814
K.G. Saur, Reed Reference Publishing Company
121 Chanlon Road, Box 31
New Providence, NJ 07974-9903
(908) 464-6800, (800) 521-8110 voice
(908) 665-6688 fax

The directories listed below are available from Gale Research Inc. Some are also available on diskette, magnetic tape, CD-ROM, or online. For further information, contact:

>Gale Research Inc.
>835 Penobscot Building
>Detroit, MI 48226
>(313) 961-2242, (800) 877-4253 voice
>(313) 961-6083 fax

Companies International
Consumer Europe
Craighead's International Business, Travel and Relocation Directory
Directory of European Industrial and Trade Associations
Directory of International Corporate Giving in America and Abroad
Encyclopedia of Associations — International Organizations
Encyclopedia of Business Information Sources: Europe
Europa World Year Book
European Advertising, Marketing, and Media Data Statistics
The European Book World
European Business Rankings
European Business Services Directory
The European Commission
European Consultants Directory
European Directory of Medium Sized Companies
European Drinks Marketing Directory
The European Food Marketing Directory
European Marketing Data and Statistics
European Wholesalers and Distributors Directory
International Brands and Their Companies
International Directory of Company Histories

International Foundation Directory
International Research Centers Directory
Major Companies of Europe
Major Chemical and Petrochemical Companies of Europe
Major Energy Companies of Europe
Major Financial Institutions of Continental Europe
Trade Shows Worldwide
Treaty of Maastricht
World Business Directory
World Directory of Trade Fairs and Exhibitions
World Market Share Reporter
World Retail Directory and Sourcebook
Worldwide Branch Locations of Multinational Companies
Worldwide Franchise Directory

The sources listed below are available online, on CD-ROM, and in hard copy from:

> Europe Information Service
> Rue de Geneve 6
> B-1140 Brussels, Belgium
> (011-322) 242-6020 voice
> (011-322) 242-9549 fax

Europe Energy
Europe Environment
European Report
European Social Policy
Multinational Service
Tech Europe
Transport Europe

The online databases listed below are available through:

> Dialog Information Services, Inc.
> 3460 Hiliview Avenue
> P. O. Box 10010, Palo Alto, CA 94303-0993
> (800) 334-2564 voice

Agence France Presse English Wire

Company Intelligence
Corporate Affiliations
Datamonitor Market Research
D & B - European Dun's Market Identifiers
Delphes European Business
Derwent World Patents Index
EIU: Business International
Euromonitor Market Research
European Patents Fulltext
Extel International Financial Cards
Extel International News Cards
Financial Times Full Text
FINDEX
Freedonia Market Research
Hoppenstedt Directory of German Companies
ICC British Company Annual Reports
ICC British Company Directory
ICC British Company Financial ~Datasheets
ICC International Business Research
IHS International Standards and Specifications
IMSworld Patents International
Infomat International Business
Investext
Kompass Europe
Kompass UK
Moody's Corporate News - International
PAIS International
PTS F & S Index
PTS International Forecasts
PTS Newsletter Database
PTS PROMPT
Research Centers and Services Directory
Reuters
Selected Data-Star Databases

Other relevant online databases include:

Amadeus
SARITEL
SpA Sarin Telematica
SS 148 Pontina KM 29 100
Pomezia 00040 Italy
(39 6) 911 971

Automated Credit Enquiry - ACE
Infolink Ltd.
Coombe Cross 2-4 South End
Croydon CRO lDL, United Kingdom
(44 816) 867 777

Business Direction
British Telecommunications PLC
81 Newgate Street
London, England ECLA 7AJ
(44 713) 564 569

Disclosure/Worldscope
Disclosure, Inc.
5161 River Road
Bethesda, MD 20816
(301) 951-1300

Europe's Largest Companies Database
ELC International
Sinclair House
The Avenue
West Ealing
London, Greater London, England W13 8NT
(44 719) 988 812

Jordans Company Information
Jordan House
47 Brunswick Place
London, England N1 6EE
(44 712) 533 030

PFDS
Achilles House
Western Avenue
London, England W3 OUA
(44 819) 923 456

WorldWide Companies (WWC)
Bahnhofstrasse 27a
P. O. Box 1323
Unterfhring, Germany D-8043
(49 89) 950-6095

PARTIAL LISTING OF OVERSEAS ELECTRONICS DIRECTORIES

APPENDIX VI

This information was provided by Ron Daniels of Miller Freeman, Inc. and Peter L. Grieco, Jr. of Professionals for Technology.

'96 -'97 Directory Electronics & Electrical Manufacturers in Korea
Electronic Industries Association of Korea
#648 Yeogsam-Dong, Kangnam-Ku, Seoul, Korea
(02) 553-0941/7 voice
(02) 555-6195, 564-7471 fax

Singapore Electronics Trade Directory '96 -'97
Singapore Information Services Pte. Ltd.
#12-03, World Trade Centre, Singapore 0409
Republic of Singapore
(65) 272-3390 voice
(65) 278-3391 fax

Korea Electronics Buyers' Guide (KEBG) '96 -'97
Korea Electronic Industries Cooperative
925-9, Bangbae I-Dong, Seoche-Ku, Seoul, 137-061 Korea
(02) 597-1010, 597-9417 voice
(02) 597-9419 fax

Republic of China: A Reference Book
Hilit Publishing Company, Ltd.
Publishers Distribution Services
6893 Sullivan Road, Grawn, MI 49637 USA
(616) 276-5196 voice
(616) 276-5197 fax

Hong Kong Trade Development Council
Courvoisier Centre II, Suite 509
601 Brickell Key Drive
Miami, FL 33131 USA
(305) 577-0414 voice
(305) 372-9142 fax

Software Rating Summary

	GOOD	FAIR	POOR	WGT,	TTL.
1. Meet requirements?	___	___	___	___	___
2. Price	___	___	___	___	___
3. Current user satisfaction	___	___	___	___	___
4. Training	___	___	___	___	___
5. Technical support	___	___	___	___	___
6. How long has current version been out?	2yr>	1-2	<1		
	___	___	___	___	___

---

7. Years company has   5yr>   2-5   0-2
   been in business   ___   ___   ___   ___   ___

8. How much modification   Little   Some   Much
   is required to meet needs? ___   ___   ___   ___   ___

9. Size of installed   10,000+   1,000s   100s
   user base   ___   ___   ___   ___   ___

10. Compatibility with
    existing software   ___   ___   ___   ___   ___

                                           TOTAL ___

Memory requirements: _____

Disk space requirements: _____

Other special requirements:

Comments:

Hardware Rating Summary

	GOOD	FAIR	POOR	WGT,	TTL.
1. Meet requirements?	___	___	___	___	___
2. Price	___	___	___	___	___
3. Current user satisfaction	___	___	___	___	___
4. Training/tech. support	___	___	___	___	___
5. How long has current version been out?	2yr> ___	1-2 ___	<1 ___		
6. Years company has been in business	5yr> ___	2-5 ___	0-2 ___	___	___
7. How much modification is required to meet needs?	Little ___	Some ___	Much ___	___	___
8. Size of installed user base	10,000+ ___	1,000s ___	100s ___	___	___
10. Warranty/maintenance	___	___	___	___	___
10. Compatibility with existing software	___	___	___	___	___

TOTAL ___

PT Publications also offers several other evaluation tools you can use:

Supply Management Toolbox by Peter L. Grieco, Jr.

How to Conduct Supplier Surveys and Audits by Janet L. Przirembel

Supplier Surveys and Audits Forms Software developed by Professionals for Technology

PARTIAL LISTING OF INTERNET ADDRESSES OF INTEREST TO BUYERS

APPENDIX VIII

Note: The author invites buyers to submit Internet addresses they think may be useful to other buyers to his email address (76353.2035@compuserve.com). This listing will be updated periodically and posted on International Purchasing Service's Web site (http://www.ipserv.com).

N.A.P.M. And Affiliates

N.A.P.M. - Tempe (http://www.napm.org)

N.A.P.M. - Carolinas/Virginia (http://www.interdyne.com/napm-car-va)

N.A.P.M. - New Orleans (http://www.gnofn.org)

N.A.P.M. - New York (http://www.solcon.com/napm-ny)

N.A.P.M. - San Diego (http://members.aol.com/napmsd/napmsd.htm)

N.A.P.M. - San Fernando Valley (http://www.loop.com/%7Enapmsfv)

N.A.P.M. - Silicon Valley - a benchmark Web page for other affiliate (http://www.catalog.com/napmsv)

N.A.P.M. - Wichita (http://www.feist.com/%Enapmw)

Other Professional Organizations

APICS - (http://www.industry.net/c/orgindex/apics)

N.I.G.P. - Nat. Instit. Govt. Purchasers - (http://www.nigp.org/nigp/)

N.C.M.A - Nat. Contract Mgt. Assoc. - (http://www.cyberserv.com/ncma/)

Purchasing Training

Professionals for Technology, Inc. (http://www.protech-inc.com/)

Publishing

PT Publications, Inc. (http://www.ptpub.com)

General

800 Directory Listings (http://www.tollfree.alt.net/dir 800/)

Internet White Pages (http://www.switchboard.com)

Internet Yellow Pages (http://www.mcp.com)

Commerce Net - consortium of companies chartered to increase commerce on the Internet (http://www.commerce.net)

Electronic Buyers News (http://techweb.cmp//ebn/)

Industry Net - database of products and companies (http://www.industry.net)

Internet White Pages (http://www.switchboard.com)

Internet Yellow Pages (http://www.mcp.com)

NAFTA / GATT Information (http://www.nafta.net)

Thomas Registers - Thomas Catalogs (http://www.thomasregister.com)

Data Security

Cyber Cash - digital payment (http://www.cybercash.com)

DigiCash - digital currency (http://www.digicash.com)

First Virtual - digital payment (http://www.fv.com)

RSA Data Security - data security (http://www.rsa.com)

Veri Sign - digital signature verification (http://www.verisign.com)

Viacrypt - PGP data security (602) 944-0773

Internet EDI Conduits

GE Information Services (http://www.ge.com)

Premenos Corp. (http://www.premenos.com)

Commercial Information Providers (Fees May Apply)

Knight-Rider Information/Dialog - includes D & B reports
      (http://www.dialog.com)

Knight-Rider Information/DataStar - European version of Dialog
      (http://www.rs.ch)

Dow Jones News/Retrieval - includes Wall Street Journal online
      (http://bis.dowjones.com)

Search Engines

Alta Vista (http://altavista.digital.com)

Excite (http://www.excite.com)

Infoseek (http://guide.infoseek.com)

Lycos (http://www.lycos.com)

Open Text (http://www.opentext.com)

Savvy Search - combines other search engines
      (http://cage.cs.colostate.edu:1969/)

WebCrawler (http://webcrawler.com)

Yahoo! (http://www.yahoo.com)

Intelligent Agents

Quarterdeck WebCompass (http://www.quarterdeck.com)

Surfbot (http://www.specter.com)

U.S. Government

Department of Commerce (http://www.doc.gov/)

Department of State (http://www.state.gov/)

Small Business Administration (http://www.sbaonline.sba.gov)

Treasury Department (http://www.ustreas.gov)

White House (http://www.whitehouse.gov)

BIBLIOGRAPHY

Bales, William A. and Feron, Harold E., "CEOs'/President's Perceptions and Expectations," *CAPS*, National Association of Purchasing Management, Tempe, AZ, 1993.

Casillas, Raul, "Foreign Sourcing: Is It For You?," *Pacific Purchaser*, Nov.-Dec. 1988.

Day, George and Wensley, Robin, "Marketing Theory with a Strategic Orientation," *Journal of Marketing*, Vol. 47, Fall 1983.

"Diversify your Supplier Base," *Insights*, National Association of Purchasing Management, Tempe, AZ, Nov. 1994.

Department of Commerce, http://www.doc.gov.

Department of State, http://www.state.gov.

Dobler, Donald and Lee, Burt, *Purchasing and Supply Management*, *6th ed.*, McGraw-Hill, New York, NY 1996.

Egan, Gerald, "Hard Times: Contracts, (growing trend of temporary employment) (What's in Store for Employee Contracts)," *Management Today*, Management Publications, Ltd., UK, January 1994.

Grieco, Jr., Peter L., and Cooper, Carl R., *Power Purchasing: Supply Management in the 21st Century*, PT Publications, West Palm Beach, FL, 1995.

Grieco, Jr., Peter L. and Hine, Paul G., *The World of Negotiations: Never Being a Loser*, PT Publications, West Palm Beach, FL, 1991.

Harding, Mary Lu, "Calculating Unit Total Cost," *Purchasing Today*, National Association of Purchasing Management, Tempe, AZ, May 1996.

Harding, Mary Lu, "Pieces of the Puzzle," *Purchasing Today*, National Association of Purchasing Management, Tempe, AZ, July 1996.

Monczka, Robert and Giunipero, Larry, *Purchasing Internationally*, Bookcrafters, Chelsea, MI, 1990.

OAS Overview of the North American Free Trade Agreement, http://www.nafta.net/naftagre.htm.

Ritterskamp, Jr., James J. and King, Donald D., Purchasing Manager's Desk Book of Purchasing Law, 2nd ed., Prentice Hall, New York, 1993.

Sharland, Alex and Giunipero, Larry, "International Outsourcing: A Current Analysis," *N.A.P.M. 79th Annual International Purchasing Conference Proceedings*, National Association of Purchasing Management, Tempe, AZ, 1994.

Small Business Administration, http://www.sbaonline.sba.gov

Williamson, Oliver, *The Economic Institutions of Capitalism*, Boston Free Press, Boston, MA 1985.

Additional Purchasing Resources from PT Publications, Inc.
3109 45th Street, Suite 100
West Palm Beach, FL 33407-1915
1-800-272-4335

The Purchasing Encyclopedia

Just-In-Time Purchasing: In Pursuit of Excellence $29.95
   Peter L. Grieco, Jr., Michael W. Gozzo and Jerry W. Claunch
Glossary of Key Purchasing Terms, Acronyms, $14.95
   and Formulas
   PT Publications
Supplier Certification II: A Handbook for $49.95
   Achieving Excellence through Continuous Improvement
   Peter L. Grieco, Jr.
World Class: Measuring Its Achievement $39.95
   Peter L. Grieco, Jr.

Purchasing Performance Measurements: A Roadmap For Excellence Mel Pilachowski	$12.95
The World Of Negotiations: Never Being a Loser Peter L. Grieco, Jr. and Paul G. Hine	$39.95
How To Conduct Supplier Surveys and Audits Janet L. Przirembel	$14.95
Supply Management Toolbox: How to Manage Your Suppliers Peter L. Grieco, Jr.	$26.95
Purchasing Capital Equipment Thomas E. Petroski	$14.95
Power Purchasing: Supply Management in the 21st Century Peter L. Grieco, Jr. and Carl R. Cooper	$39.95
Global Sourcing Lee Krotseng	$14.95
Purchasing Ethics Jim Rhodes	$14.95
Purchasing Contract Law, UCC, and Patents Mark Grieco	$14.95
EDI Purchasing: The Electronic Gateway to the Future Steven Marks	$14.95
Site Smart Purchasing Craig A. Melby and Jane Utzman	$14.95
MRO Purchasing Peter L. Grieco, Jr.	$14.95
The Complete Guide to Contracts Management For Facilities Services John P. Mahoney and Linda S. Keckler	$18.95
The Complete Guide to Contracts Management For Components John P. Mahoney and Linda S. Keckler	$23.95
The Complete Guide to Contracts Management For Promotional Services William F. Badenhoff and John P. Mahoney	$18.95

The Complete Guide to Contracts Management For Business Practices William F. Badenhoff and John P. Mahoney	$23.95
The Complete Guide to Contracts Management For Office Services John P. Mahoney and William F. Badenhoff	$16.95
The Complete Guide to Contracts Management For Peripherals John P. Mahoney and William F. Badenhoff	$23.95
The Complete Guide to Contracts Management For Capital Equipment John P. Mahoney and William F. Badenhoff	$14.95
The Complete Guide to Contracts Management For Human Resources Services John P. Mahoney and Linda S. Keckler	$16.95
The Complete Guide to Contracts Management For Security Services William F. Badenhoff and John P. Mahoney	$16.95
The Complete Guide to Contracts Management For Contract Manufacturing John P. Mahoney and William F. Badenhoff	$23.95
The Complete Guide to Contracts Management For Distributors John P. Mahoney and William F. Badenhoff	$18.95
The Complete Guide to Contracts Management For Transportation and Logistics Services Volume 1 John P. Mahoney and Linda S. Keckler	$18.95
The Complete Guide to Contracts Management For Transportation and Logistics Services Volume 2 John P. Mahoney and Linda S. Keckler	$18.95
The Complete Guide to Contracts Management For Travel Services John P. Mahoney and Linda S. Keckler	$16.95

Purchasing Video Education Series

Supplier Certification The Path to Excellence
Tape 1: Why Supplier Certification?	$395.00
Tape 2: Quality at the Supplier	$395.00
Tape 3: How to Select a Supplier	$395.00
Tape 4: Supplier Surveys and Audits	$395.00
Tape 5: Supplier Quality Agreements	$395.00
Tape 6: Supplier Ratings	$395.00
Tape 7: Phases of Supplier Certification	$395.00

Tape 8: Implementing a Supplier Certification Program
$395.00

Tape 9: Evaluating Your Supplier Certification Program
$395.00

Complete Nine Tape Series $1,995.00

Purchasing Audio Tapes

The World of Negotiations: How to Win Every Time $39.95

Purchasing Software

Supplier Survey and Audit Forms $395.00
Developed by Professionals For Technology Associates, Inc.

ContractWare™
Developed by The Leadership Companies, Inc.

Business Practices	$599.00
Capital Equipment	$599.00
Components	$599.00
Peripherals	$599.00
Contract Manufacturing	$599.00
Distributors	$599.00

Facilities Management	$599.00
Human Resources	$599.00
Office Services	$599.00
Promotional Services	$599.00
Security Services	$599.00
Transportation and Logistics	$599.00
Travel Services	$599.00

Site License (unlimited users per site)	Call
Corporate License (unlimited users, unlimited sites)	Call
Administrative Library Database (requires site of corporate license)	Call

CyberBase™
Client Server Software containing all 14 contract families
Developed by the Leadership Companies, Inc.

Individual Server Licenses	Call
Corporate License (unlimited servers, unlimited users)	Call
Additional Installations	Call

Additional Professional Textbooks

Failure Modes and Effects Analysis: Predicting and Preventing Problems Before They Occur Paul Palady	$39.95
Made In America: The Total Business Concept Peter L. Grieco, Jr. and Michael W. Gozzo	$29.95
Reengineering Through Cycle Time Management Wayne L. Douchkoff and Thomas E. Petroski	$39.95
Behind Bars: Bar Coding Principles and Applications Peter L. Grieco, Jr., Michael W. Gozzo and C. J. (Chip) Long	$39.95
People Empowerment: Achieving Success from Involvement Michael W. Gozzo and Wayne L. Douchkoff	$39.95
Activity Based Costing: The Key to World Class Performance Peter L. Grieco, Jr. and Mel Pilachowski	$18.00

INDEX

A
Activity Based Costing (ABC) 7
Agents 42
Approved supplier list 53

B
Best cost 8
Bidding process 53-54
Business Information Centers (BICs) 71-78
Buy American 12

C
Centralized vs. decentralized purchasing 18
Commission houses 41
Competitive bidding 55-56
Contracts for the International Sale of Goods (CISG) 33
Cost analysis 63-65
Customs forms 31

D

E

F

G

I